G.B. Royal Academy of Arts

Winter Exhibition

G.B. Royal Academy of Arts

Winter Exhibition

ISBN/EAN: 9783337255794

Printed in Europe, USA, Canada, Australia, Japan

Cover: Foto ©Thomas Meinert / pixelio.de

More available books at **www.hansebooks.com**

EXHIBITION

OF

WORKS BY

VAN DYCK

1599–1641

WINTER EXHIBITION

THIRTY-FIRST YEAR

MDCCCC

LONDON

PRINTED BY WM. CLOWES AND SONS, LIMITED, 14 CHARING CROSS

PRINTERS TO THE ROYAL ACADEMY

The Exhibition opens on Monday, January 1st, and closes on Saturday, March 10th.

Hours of Admission from 9 A.M. till 6 P.M.

Price of Admission, 1s.

Price of Catalogue, 6d.

Season Ticket, 5s.

General Index to the Catalogues of the first twenty Exhibitions, in two parts; Part I. 1870–1879, 2s.; Part II. 1880–1889, 1s. 6d.

No sticks, umbrellas or parasols are allowed to be taken into the Galleries. They must be given up to the attendants at the Cloak Room in the Entrance Hall. The other attendants are strictly forbidden to take charge of anything.

The Refreshment Room is reached by the staircase leading out of the Water Colour Room.

The Gibson (Sculpture) Gallery and the Diploma Galleries are open daily, from 11 A.M. to 4 P.M. Admission free. Entrance by the door at the east end of the portico.

All Communications should be addressed to " The Secretary."

CONTENTS.

	PAGE
SHORT BIOGRAPHICAL NOTICE OF VAN DYCK	5

Oil Paintings—

	PAGE
GALLERY I.	9
„ II.	14
„ III.	22
, IV.	31
„ V.	37
„ VI.	43

Oil Sketches and Drawings—

	PAGE
WATER COLOUR ROOM	48
INDEX OF THE NAMES OF CONTRIBUTORS OF WORKS	60

PLAN OF THE GALLERIES.

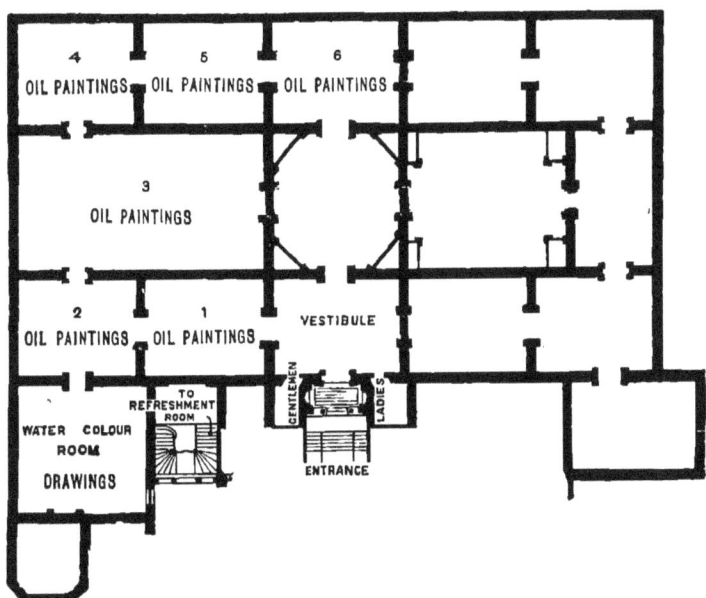

ROYAL ACADEMY OF ARTS IN LONDON, 1900.

HONORARY MEMBERS.

THE MOST REV. W. D. MACLAGAN, D.D., LORD ARCHBISHOP OF YORK, *Chaplain.*
PROFESSOR R. C. JEBB, M.P., *Professor of Ancient History.*
THE RT. REV. M. CREIGHTON, D.D., BISHOP OF LONDON, *Professor of Ancient Literature.*
FRANCIS C. PENROSE, ESQ., *Antiquary.*
THE RT. HON. WM. E. H. LECKY, M.P., *Secretary for Foreign Correspondence.*

HONORARY RETIRED ACADEMICIANS.

FAED, THOMAS, ESQ.
FRITH, WILLIAM POWELL, ESQ.
HORSLEY, JOHN CALLCOTT, ESQ.

PICKERSGILL, FREDK. RICH., ESQ
WATTS, GEORGE FREDERICK, ESQ.

HONORARY FOREIGN ACADEMICIANS.

BRETON, JULES.
DUBOIS, PAUL.

GÉRÔME, JEAN LÉON.
GUILLAUME, CLAUDE J. B. E.

KNAUS, LUDWIG.
MENZEL, ADOLF.

ACADEMICIANS.

ABBEY, EDWIN A., ESQ.
AITCHISON, GEORGE, ESQ.
ALMA-TADEMA, SIR LAWRENCE.
ARMSTEAD, HENRY HUGH, ESQ.
BOUGHTON, GEORGE H., ESQ.
BROCK, THOMAS, ESQ.
COOPER, THOMAS SIDNEY, ESQ.
CROFTS, ERNEST, ESQ., *Keeper and Trustee.*
DAVIS, HENRY WM. BANKS, ESQ.
DICKSEE, FRANK, ESQ., *Auditor.*
FILDES, LUKE, ESQ.
FORD, EDWARD ONSLOW, ESQ.
GILBERT, ALFRED, ESQ., M.V.O.
GOODALL, FREDERICK, ESQ.
GOW, ANDREW C., ESQ.
GRAHAM, PETER, ESQ.
GREGORY, EDWARD JOHN, ESQ.
HERKOMER, HUBERT, ESQ.
HOOK, JAMES CLARKE, ESQ.
JACKSON, THOMAS GRAHAM, ESQ., *Auditor.*
LESLIE, GEORGE DUNLOP, ESQ.

LEADER, BENJ. WILLIAMS, ESQ.
LUCAS, JOHN SEYMOUR, ESQ.
MACWHIRTER, JOHN, ESQ.
ORCHARDSON, WILLIAM QUILLER, ESQ.
OULESS, WALTER WILLIAM, ESQ.
POYNTER, SIR EDWARD J., *President and Trustee.*
PRINSEP, VALENTINE CAMERON, ESQ.
RICHMOND, SIR WILLIAM BLAKE, K.C.B.
RIVIERE, BRITON, ESQ., *Trustee.*
SANT, JAMES, ESQ.
SARGENT, JOHN SINGER, ESQ.
SHAW, RICHARD NORMAN, ESQ.
STONE, MARCUS, ESQ.
THORNYCROFT, W. HAMO, ESQ.
WATERHOUSE, ALFRED, ESQ., *Treasurer and Trustee.*
WATERHOUSE, JOHN WILLIAM, ESQ.
WELLS, HENRY TANWORTH, ESQ., *Auditor.*
WOODS, HENRY, ESQ.
YEAMES, WILLIAM FREDERICK, ESQ., *Librarian.*

HONORARY RETIRED ASSOCIATES.

LE JEUNE, HENRY.
NICOL, ERSKINE.
STACPOOLE, FREDERICK.

ASSOCIATES.

BATES, HARRY.
BODLEY, GEORGE FREDERICK.
BRAMLEY, FRANK.
BRETT, JOHN.
CLAUSEN, GEORGE.
COPE, ARTHUR STOCKDALE.
CROWE, EYRE.
EAST, ALFRED.
FORBES, STANHOPE A.
FRAMPTON, GEORGE JAMES.

HACKER, ARTHUR.
HEMY, CHAS. NAPIER.
HUNTER, COLIN.
JOHN, WILLIAM GOSCOMBE.
LA THANGUE, HERBERT HENRY.
MACBETH, ROBERT WALKER.
MORRIS, PHILIP RICHARD.
MURRAY, DAVID.
NORTH, JOHN WILLIAM.

PARSONS, ALFRED.
SHANNON, JAMES J.
SMYTHE, LIONEL PERCY.
SOLOMON, SOLOMON J.
STOREY, GEORGE ADOLPHUS.
SWAN, JOHN MCALLAN.
WATERLOW, ERNEST ALBERT
WEBB, ASTON.
WYLLIE, WILLIAM LIONEL.

PROFESSORS.

Of *Painting,* HUBERT HERKOMER, ESQ., R.A.
Of *Sculpture,* vacant.

Of *Architecture,* GEO. AITCHISON, ESQ., R.A.
Of *Anatomy,* WILLIAM ANDERSON, F.R.C.S.
Of *Chemistry,* A. H. CHURCH, M.A., F.R.S.

Teacher of *Perspective,*
Master of the Architectural School, R. PHENÉ SPIERS.

SECRETARY—FRED. A. EATON.

ANTHONY VAN DYCK.

BORN 1599. DIED 1641.

———◦◇◦———

ANTHONY VAN DYCK was born on March 22, 1599, at Antwerp, where his
family had been settled for several generations. Both his grandfather and
father were merchants; the latter, whose name was Frans, being evi-
dently a man of position and means, as he held the important office of
director of the Chapel of the Holy Sacrament in the Cathedral. Frans van
Dyck's first wife died in childbirth soon after their marriage, and he
then took as his second wife Marie Cupers, or Cuypers, who bore him twelve
children, of whom Anthony was the seventh. While the father appears to
have had no interests beyond his business and the discharge of his religious
duties, the mother is said to have been a person of much taste and greatly
interested in everything connected with art. From her, no doubt, the great
artist derived many of those qualities for which his works are conspicuous.

After the death of his mother, which took place when he was eight years
old, he remained at home for two or three years, and then, in 1610, entered
as an apprentice the studio of Hendrick van Balen, who was considered
one of the first artists of the day. Two years later he became a pupil
of Rubens, with whom he worked for about six years. His admission
into the studio of that painter at the early age of thirteen is, of itself, a
testimony to his precocious talent, as Rubens was then at the height of his
fame, and is known to have refused hundreds of pupils who flocked to him
from all parts, while artists whose reputation was already made came to
profit by the teaching and the advice of their illustrious colleague.
Admitted in 1618 into the Guild of St. Luke, Van Dyck soon was acknow-

ledged as the chief and most distinguished of Rubens' pupils, and was associated with him in the execution of many important works. His name, indeed, was already known beyond the borders of his own country, and in 1620, at the invitation of the famous connoisseur the Earl of Arundel, he came to England and painted some portraits, among them one of the King, James I. His stay in England, however, was very short, and early in 1621 he returned to Antwerp and resumed his connection with Rubens, assisting him probably in the great work of decorating the Church of the Jesuits. Towards the end of that year, urged thereto by his master, he set out for Italy, stopping on the journey at Saventhem, near Brussels, to paint for the church of that village the famous picture of " St. Martin dividing his cloak with the Beggar," of which there is another version at Windsor Castle till lately attributed to Rubens.

Van Dyck arrived at Genoa in November and, thanks to his own personal attractions and the friendship of the brothers Lucas and Cornelius de Wael, Flemish artists resident in that town, he soon met with great success as a portrait painter. In Italy he remained four years, spending most of the time at Genoa, but visiting many other towns, Florence, Venice, Turin, Mantua, etc., and staying some months at Rome where he painted several portraits, among them that of the Cardinal Bentivoglio in the Pitti Palace at Florence, and also some religious subjects. It is said, indeed, that during the four years of his sojourn in Italy he executed no less than 100 pictures. Quitting Genoa in June 1625, he went by the littoral of the Mediterranean through France to Paris, where he remained a short time, reaching Antwerp at the end of 1625 or beginning of 1626.

The next few years of Van Dyck's life were passed almost entirely in his native country, with occasional visits to Brussels and other places, for the purpose of painting certain portraits. He is also said to have paid short visits to London and Paris in 1627. During the whole of this period the industry and energy he had already displayed showed no abatement. Pictures, chiefly religious, and portraits followed one another from his brush with amazing rapidity, and his fame was second only to that of Rubens.

But, notwithstanding all this activity and success, he does not appear to have reached in his native town, either in consideration or wealth, the com-

manding position of his sometime master. Was it a sense of this inferiority
which induced him to listen to the proposals of his many English admirers,
the chief among them the Earl of Arundel, that he should come to England
and place himself under the protection of Charles I., who was eager to accord
him patronage? At any rate he accepted the invitation, and in April 1632,
arrived in London and took up his residence in a house in Blackfriars, being
also provided with summer apartments in the King's House at Eltham.
Charles immediately made him "Principal Painter in Ordinary to their
Majesties," and on July 5, three months after his arrival, conferred upon him
the honour of knighthood.

From that time onward his career was one of almost unexampled success,
marred only by gradually failing health arising, it is said, from the constant
drain upon his strength caused by his mode of life and by the unintermitting
labours necessary to procure the means for gratifying his luxurious tastes.
By the King he was given constant employment. Without counting the
numerous portraits of Charles and of Queen Henrietta Maria in private
collections and galleries abroad, there are said to be in England seven
equestrian portraits and seventeen full lengths or half lengths of the
monarch, and twenty-five of his queen. But it was not the Royal family
only that provided employment for the prolific pencil of Van Dyck. Every-
one of distinction in England desired to have his or her features immortalised
by the courtly and popular painter, with the result that some three hundred
portraits, more or less the work of his hand, exist in this country.

With the exception of a visit to Antwerp and Brussels in 1634, Van Dyck
remained in England till 1640, in which year, or the preceding one—the date
is uncertain—he married Mary Ruthven (No. 80), urged thereto by King
Charles, who hoped by this means to check his extravagant expenditure, and
effect a change in those habits of life which were gradually undermining his
constitution. But it was too late. After a journey abroad with his wife
during the end of 1640 and the beginning of 1641, he returned to England a
dying man, and though everything that the medical science of the day could
suggest was done—the King offering three hundred pounds to any doctor who
could save his life—he expired in his house at Blackfriars on December 9,
1641, at the early age of forty-two. Two days after he was buried in the old

Cathedral of St. Paul's, near the tomb of John of Gaunt, and a monument was erected over him with the following inscription : "Qui dum viveret multis immortalitatem donaverat vita functus est. Carolus I. Mag. Brit. Fr. et Hib. Rex Antonio Van Dyck equiti aurato P.C." Monument and inscription both perished in the Great Fire of London which destroyed the old Cathedral.

Van Dyck's activity as a painter may be divided into four epochs:— (1) his early days at Antwerp up to the time of his journey to Italy in 1621 ; (2) his stay in that country till 1625; (3) his residence in Flanders from 1625 to 1632; (4) his life in England from 1632 till his death. Most of the pictures in this Exhibition belong to the last period, but there are a few which illustrate the brilliancy of the work done by him in Italy in the heyday of his youth, as e.g. Nos. 47, 60, 62, 70, 77, 124, and also when he had reached the full maturity of his powers on his return to his native country, as Nos. 4, 11, 36, 43, 51, 59, 66, 68, 87, 92, 99, 107, 118, and most of the religious subjects, though it is possible that Nos. 115 and 120 belong to the period before his journey to Italy. Some idea of his amazing industry and rapid execution may be gathered from the fact that the list of works attributed to him reaches the enormous total of more than one thousand.

Van Dyck hardly ever signed his pictures. Indeed, not more than fifteen or twenty canvases are supposed to bear his genuine signature. In all other cases where it exists it has been added by another hand.

CATALOGUE.

The Numbers follow from left to right.

The Portraits are described under four sizes:—"bust," the head and shoulders; "half figure," to the waist; "three-quarter figure," to the knee and below; "full length," the entire figure.

The terms "to right," "to left," and "on right," "on left," in all descriptions denote the right and left of the spectator.

The following abbreviations are used:—b. born; m. married; d. died; r. right; l. left.

In the sizes of the Works the height is always placed before the width.

GALLERY No. 1.

OIL PAINTINGS—Nos. 1-14.

LENT BY

1   Portrait of THE PRINCESS MARY when a Child.

EARL OF NORMANTON.

> Daughter of Charles I. (No. 20); b. 1631; m. 1648, William, Prince of Orange; d. 1660; her son became William III.
> Full length, standing to l., three-quarter profile, hands clasped in front; blue satin dress trimmed with silver, broad lace frill and lace apron; curtain and architectural background. Canvas, 58 by 42 in.

2   Portrait of THE EARL OF ARUNDEL.

DUKE OF SUTHERLAND.

> Thomas Howard, son of Philip, 4th Earl; b. 1592; was the first
> collector of works of art in England; the famous collection of
> inscriptions known as the Arundel Marbles was brought by him
> to England; d. 1646.
> Half figure, seated to r., in a red arm-chair, looking towards the
> spectator; in his r. hand is a scroll; his l. holds a medallion
> which is suspended by a black ribbon from his neck; black
> dress, lace ruff; curtain and landscape background. Canvas,
> 40 by 30½ in.

3   Portrait of THE EARL OF NORTHUMBERLAND, K.G.

EARL OF ESSEX.

> Algernon Percy, 10th Earl; son of the 9th Earl and Dorothy,
> sister of Robert Devereux, Earl of Essex, Queen Elizabeth's
> favourite; born 1602; Lord High Admiral; d. 1668.
> Full length, standing to r., looking towards the spectator; his r.
> hand holds a baton, his l. clasps the hilt of his sword, his foot is
> on the stock of an anchor; in armour, bare-headed; with vest
> of yellow satin, crimson breeches and buff boots; he wears the
> insignia of the Garter; in the background is represented a naval
> engagement. Canvas, 85 by 50 in.

4   Portraits of SNYDERS WITH HIS WIFE AND CHILD.

MRS. CULLING HANBURY.

> Franz Snyders, the well-known painter of still life, and afterwards
> of animals; b. at Antwerp 1579; died there 1657. His wife
> was a sister of Paul de Vos and Cornelius de Vos.
> Three-quarter figures, seated, facing the spectator; Snyders, on the
> l., leans forward with his r. hand on the arm of a chair, while
> his wife, turned slightly to l., holds on her lap the child, which
> is turning round towards its father; both are in dark dress;
> Snyders wears a lace collar and his wife a large ruff and she
> wears a gold-embroidered bodice; curtain background. Canvas,
> 63 by 48 in.

LENT BY

5				Portrait of MRS. KIRK.

EARL COWPER, K.G.

Bed-chamber woman to Queen Henrietta Maria, daughter of
Aurelian Townshend, the poet.
Full length, standing to l., pointing to l. with her r. hand; her l.
hand holds back the skirt of her amber satin gown, a brown
scarf crosses her body diagonally; in front of her is a small
dog, jumping up at a butterfly; curtain and architectural
background, with rose tree and garden on the l. Canvas,
87 by 51 in.

6				Portrait of VISCOUNT STAFFORD.

MARQUESS OF BUTE.

William Howard, 3rd son of Thomas, Earl of Arundel and Surrey,
created 1647 Viscount Stafford; he was accused in 1676 of
having taken part in the Popish Plot, and was executed in 1680.
Half figure, standing to r., his l. arm resting on his hip, and the
r. pressed upon his breast; bare-headed; black satin coat, white
falling collar; gold hilted sword; ribbon of the Bath; dark
background. Canvas, 38 by 32 in.

7				Portrait of AN ARTIST.

DUKE OF SUTHERLAND.

Three-quarter figure, seated to r., with head turned towards the
spectator, at a table on which are some papers, a globe, and a
plaster mask; in his l. hand is a pair of compasses; his r. grasps
the arm of his chair; black dress, lace collar; dark background.
Canvas, 48 by 38½ in.

8				Portrait of A MAN IN ARMOUR.

SIR SAMUEL MONTAGU, BART., M.P.

Half figure, standing to l., bare-headed, looking towards the spectator; his r. hand holds a baton, his l. rests upon his hip; under
his armour he wears a yellow and black striped dress with lace
collar, and a broad silk scarf passes over his breast; dark background with red curtain. Canvas, 49 by 39 in.

LENT BY

9 Portrait of QUEEN HENRIETTA MARIA.

CAPTAIN CHAMBERS.

See No. 20.
Half figure, standing slightly turned to l., three-quarter face, looking
at the spectator, her hands crossed in front of her; yellow satin
dress with wide lace collar and cuffs and black sash; pearl ornaments; a crown lies on a table beside her; dark background.
Canvas, 40½ by 32 in.

10 Portrait of THE MARQUESS OF HUNTLY.

DUKE OF BUCCLEUCH, K.G.

George Gordon, 2nd Marquess, son of George, 1st Marquess; was
a firm adherent of Charles I. during the Rebellion; beheaded in
consequence in 1649.
Full length, standing, bare-headed, turned slightly to r., looking
at the spectator, his r. hand resting on a stick, his l. is on his
hip; cuirass, red dress richly embroidered, wide lace collar, blue
sash embroidered with silver, buff boots; on a table behind him
is his helmet; curtain and architectural background. Canvas,
71 by 50 in.

11 Portrait of A LADY AND CHILD.

EARL BROWNLOW.

Three-quarter figure of a lady, seated to l., looking at the spectator;
on her lap she holds the child, which is holding out its arms to
l.; black satin dress over a yellow bodice, large stiff ruff, and
lace cuffs; the child is in purple silk, with a grey hat; curtain
background, with sky seen through opening to l. Canvas,
50 by 41 in.

LENT BY

**12 QUEEN HENRIETTA MARIA WITH HER DWARF,
SIR GEOFFREY HUDSON.**

EARL FITZWILLIAM, K.G.

See No. 20.

Sir Geoffrey Hudson was born in 1620; when seven years old and 30 inches high he was served up in a pie and presented to the Queen by the Duke of Buckingham; he afterwards grew to be 3 feet 9 inches; he went with the Queen to France in 1644, and while there fought a duel with a Mr. Crofts, whom he killed at the first shot; returning at the Restoration, he was imprisoned on suspicion of being engaged in the Popish Plot; d. 1682.

Full-length figures, standing on a terrace; the Queen, who occupies the centre of the picture, stands to l. looking at the spectator, and touches with her r. hand a small monkey which the dwarf holds on his l. arm; her l. hand holds a fold of her blue satin dress; she wears a wide black hat and lace collar; the dwarf is in red; on the r. are a column and red curtain; foliage and sky on the l. Canvas, 86 by 51 in.

13 Portrait of THE DUKE OF RICHMOND AND LENNOX.

MARQUESS OF BRISTOL.

James Stuart, son of Esmé, Duke of Lennox; b. 1612; created Duke of Richmond 1641; was a devoted adherent of Charles I.; d. 1655.

Half figure, standing to l., looking towards the spectator, three-quarter face; he is bare-headed, and clad in crimson breeches and white shirt, and is represented as " Paris," with an apple in his hand; long fair hair falls over his shoulders; landscape background. Canvas, 40 by 29¼ in.

14 Portrait of THE EARL OF PEMBROKE.

EARL OF PEMBROKE.

Philip, 5th Earl, 3rd son of the 4th Earl, by Susan de Vere, daughter of the 17th Earl of Oxford; d. 1669.

Three-quarter figure, standing in front, bare-headed; in cuirass and crimson dress, showing white sleeves; his r. hand holds the crimson sash which crosses his breast; his gloved l. hand, holding the other glove, rests against the hilt of his sword; long fair hair falling over his shoulders; dark background. Canvas, 51¼ by 40 in.

GALLERY No. II.

OIL PAINTINGS—Nos. 15-42.

LENT BY

15 Portrait of LORD HOWARD.

DUKE OF NORFOLK, K.G.

> Bust to l., showing r. hand gloved, head turned towards the spectator; black dress, wide white collar; long fair hair; brown background. Canvas, 28 by 22 in.

16 HOLY FAMILY.

DUKE OF BUCCLEUCH, K.G.

> Three-quarter figure of the Virgin, standing beside a stone slab, on which, with both hands, she holds the Child, and looking down at St. John, who is presenting a scroll to the Child; in front of St. John is a dog; architectural and sky background. Canvas, 60 by 43½ in.

17 Portrait of THE COUNTESS OF ARUNDEL.

DUKE OF RICHMOND AND GORDON.

> Lucy Sidney.
> Half figure to l., looking at the spectator; white satin dress, cut low and ornamented with pearls, pearl necklace and ear-rings; a fur boa is over her r. shoulder; dark background. Canvas, 29 by 24 in.

LENT BY

18   Portrait of THE DUKE OF RICHMOND AND LENNOX.

DUKE OF BUCCLEUCH, K.G.

> See No. 13.
> Full length, standing slightly to r., his r. hand holding his hat;
> black satin dress, showing white at the sleeves and breast,
> wide white collar; a black cloak with star is over his l. arm;
> he wears the insignia of the Garter; architectural and curtain
> background. Canvas, 82 by 49 in.

19   Portrait of ARCHBISHOP LAUD.

EARL FITZWILLIAM, K.G.

> William Laud, b. 1573 at Reading; Dean of Gloucester 1616;
> Bishop of St. David's 1621; Bishop of Bath and Wells 1626;
> Archbishop of Canterbury 1633; impeached by the Long
> Parliament and condemned to death 1640; beheaded 1645.
> Half figure, standing in front, leaning his r. arm on the base of a
> pillar; he is arrayed in his robes. Canvas, 51½ by 51½ in.
> (circular).

20   KING CHARLES I. AND QUEEN HENRIETTA MARIA.

DUKE OF GRAFTON, K.G.

> (1) Second son of James I.; b. 1600; executed 1649.
> (2) Daughter of Henry IV. of France and Maria de' Medici;
> b. 1609; m. Charles I. 1625; d. 1669.
> Two half figures. The King on the l. standing to r. looking at the
> Queen, with l. hand on the hilt of his sword and r. extended to
> take a wreath which she is offering him; he wears a crimson and
> white dress with wide lace collar and the ribbon of the Garter;
> on a table and behind him lies a crown. The Queen, standing
> to l., looks towards the spectator; she holds the wreath in her r.
> hand and a spray of green in her l.; she wears a white dress
> with lace and pink ribbons, and a pearl necklace and ear-rings;
> green curtains on either side, with landscape seen between them.
> Canvas, 36 by 64 in.

LENT BY

21   Portrait of LADY WENTWORTH.

EARL FITZWILLIAM, K.G.

Arabella, daughter of Holles, Earl of Clare; m., as his second
wife, 1625, · Thomas, Lord Wentworth, afterwards Earl of
Strafford (see No. 49).

Full length, standing to l., with one foot on a step at the foot of a
pillar, looking towards the spectator; with her r. hand she is
putting aside a curtain, while with her l. she holds up her
skirt; blue satin dress with jewels, cut very low, and the sleeve
fastened back to show the gold embroidery inside, pearl necklace and ear-rings; garden seen to r. Canvas, 85 by 50 in.

22   ST. MARTIN DIVIDING HIS CLOAK.

CAPTAIN G. L. HOLFORD.

Small figure of the saint, mounted on a white horse, in the act of
dividing his cloak and giving part of it to a half-naked beggar
as he rides through a gateway past various figures of beggars,
&c.; he is followed by other horsemen. Panel, 13 by 10 in.

Sketch for the large picture at Windsor.

23   THE MIRACLE OF ST. BENEDICT.

EARL OF NORMANTON.

A pope and a young king in armour, kneeling on the steps of an
altar; in the foreground, groups of plague-stricken men, women
and children; sketch. Panel, 21 by 15½ in.

24   VIRGIN AND CHILD.

LADY DE ROTHSCHILD.

Three-quarter figure of the Virgin, seated to l., holding the Child
on her lap; He is holding up His r. hand, in the attitude of
benediction, towards the donor, who kneels on the l., with hands
joined; curtain and sky background. Canvas, 41½ by 46 in.
(oval).

This picture probably represents the Duchess d'Aremberg and her
infant son in the characters of the Virgin and Child, and the
Abbé Scaglia (No. 66) as the donor.

25   Portrait of A LADY.

ALFRED J. SANDERS, ESQ.

> Said to represent the Countess of Oxford.
> Half figure to l., looking at the spectator; black, low-cut dress,
> pearl necklace and ear-rings; dark background.   Canvas,
> 28½ by 24 in.

26   Portrait of A LADY.

HENRY F. MAKINS, ESQ.

> Small full length, seated to l. in a room, looking at the spectator;
> her arms rest on the arms of the chair, and the r. hand
> holds a handkerchief; black dress, stiff white ruff and cuffs;
> she wears a chain and cross; on the r. is a column.   Panel,
> 17 by 13 in.

27   THE BAPTISM OF CHRIST.

J. T. DOBIE, ESQ.

> Small full-length figure of the Saviour, with bent head and knees,
> being baptised by St. John in the river; two angels stand near,
> and the First Person of the Trinity appears in the sky above.
> Marble, 11½ by 15¼ in.

28   Portrait of LUCIUS CARY, 2nd VISCOUNT FALKLAND.

DUKE OF DEVONSHIRE, K.G.

> The celebrated soldier, author and statesman; son of Henry,
> 1st Viscount; b. 1610; M.P. for Newport 1640; Secretary of
> State 1642; fought at Edgehill and was killed at Newbury,
> Sept. 20, 1643.
> Half figure to r., looking at the spectator; black and white dress,
> wide lace collar; long hair curling over his shoulders; dark
> background.   Canvas, 28 by 23 in.

29   Portrait of THE DUKE OF RICHMOND AND LENNOX.

EARL OF DENBIGH.

> See Nos. 13 and 18.   He is here represented with the dog which
> saved him from assassination by arousing him from sleep.
> Full length, standing to l., looking at the spectator, caressing a
> greyhound with his r. hand; his l. hand rests on his hip;

LENT BY

black dress and cloak, with star, blue stockings, black shoes,
with enormous rosettes, wide lace collar ; he wears the insignia
of the Garter ; long fair hair falling over his shoulders ; curtain
and architectural background. Canvas, 80 by 47½ in.

30   THE BETRAYAL OF CHRIST.

LORD METHUEN.

In the centre of the picture are the figures, larger than life, of the
Saviour and Judas Iscariot ; Judas, wrapped in a brown robe,
is holding the r. hand of Christ, and bending towards Him ;
numerous figures, in different attitudes, are grouped round them,
under the trees of the garden, pressing forward ; one on the l.
holds up a torch. Canvas, 107 by 88 in.

31   Portrait of THE DUCHESS OF RICHMOND AND HER DWARF MRS. GIBSON.

EARL OF DENBIGH.

Mary, daughter of George, Duke of Buckingham, and Lady
Katharine Manners ; m. first, in 1634, Sir Charles Herbert ;
secondly, James, Duke of Richmond and Lennox (Nos. 13, 18
and 29) ; thirdly, Thomas Howard ; d. 1685.

Mrs. Gibson was wife of Richard Gibson, an artist and also a
dwarf.

Full length, standing to l., with one foot on a step, on which
Mrs. Gibson is standing ; her r. hand is taking a glove from a
salver, which is held up to her by the dwarf ; her l. holds a fold
of her skirt ; blue dress, cut low, with flowing sleeves turned
back to show a crimson lining, and ornamented with pearls,
pearl necklace and ear-rings. Mrs. Gibson wears a dress of red
velvet. Architectural background ; landscape seen through an
opening to l. Canvas, 81 by 48 in.

32   Portrait of COLONEL CHARLES CAVENDISH.

DUKE OF DEVONSHIRE, K.G.

2nd son of William Cavendish, 2nd Earl of Devonshire, by
Christian, daughter of Edward, Lord Bruce of Kinross ; b. 1620 ;
travelled a good deal ; became a soldier and fought at Edgehill ;
killed in action in 1643.

Half figure to l., looking at the spectator ; black and white dress,
very large white lace collar ; long brown hair curling over his
shoulders ; dark background. Canvas, 27½ by 22½ in.

LENT BY

33   Portrait of LADY CAPEL.

EARL OF CLARENDON.

> Elizabeth, daughter of Sir Charles Morrison, of Cassiobury; m.
> Arthur, son of Sir H. Capel, afterwards, 1641, created Baron
> Capel (No. 123).
> Half figure to l., looking at the spectator; pink satin dress, with
> lace kerchief covering the neck and shoulders; brown back-
> ground. Canvas, 29¼ by 23¼ in.

34   A HORSE.

EARL BROWNLOW.

> Study of a white horse in a landscape. Sketch. Canvas, 32¼ by
> 27½ in.

35   Portrait of THE PAINTER.

THE LATE DUKE OF WESTMINSTER, K.G.

> See notice at the beginning of the Catalogue.
> Bust to r., showing both hands, his head turned back towards the
> spectator; his r. hand points to a sunflower, while his l. holds
> a gold chain, which passes over his r. shoulder; crimson dress;
> long auburn hair; sky background. Canvas, 23¼ by 29 in.

36   Portrait of THE CARDINAL FERDINAND.

EARL OF CLARENDON.

> Ferdinand of Austria, son of Philip III. of Spain and Margaret of
> Austria; b. 1609; created a Cardinal in 1619; was appointed
> Governor of the Low Countries at the death of his aunt, the
> Infanta Isabella Clara Eugenia in 1633; d. 1641.
> Half figure to l., looking at the spectator; red and gold dress,
> with broad sash across his breast; wide white lace collar; dark
> background. Canvas, 32¼ by 28 in.

LENT BY

37   Portrait of KING CHARLES I.

DUKE OF NORFOLK, K.G.

See No. 20.
Half figure, full face, in armour; his r. hand holds a baton, his l.
arm rests on a helmet which lies on a table beside him; a crown
is beside the helmet; brown background. Canvas, 39½ by 32 in.

38   Portraits of GEORGE AND FRANCIS VILLIERS.

H.M. THE QUEEN.
(From Windsor Castle.)

Sons of George Villiers, 1st Duke of Buckingham.
(1) George; b. 1627; succeeded as 2nd Duke 1628; fought at
Worcester 1651; became principal minister 1667; killed the
Earl of Shrewsbury in a duel; d. 1687.
(2) Francis; b. 1629; "the beautiful Francis Villiers"; killed
while engaged in a rising on behalf of the King in 1648, in a
lane between Surbiton and Kingston; buried in Henry VII.'s
Chapel.
Full lengths of two boys, standing facing the spectator. On the l.
(1) in crimson dress, with crimson cloak over his r. arm, which
rests on his hip. On the r. (2) looking to l., in yellow dress
and cloak, his gloved r. hand held against his breast, his l. at
his side. Both have long hair falling over wide lace collars.
Architectural and curtain background. Canvas, 59 by 49 in.

39   Portrait of QUEEN HENRIETTA MARIA.

LORD WANTAGE.

See No. 20.
Half figure, standing to l, looking at the spectator; her r. hand
rests on some roses which lie on a table beside her, her l.
holds a fold of her gown; white satin gown with lace and pink
bows, pearl necklace and ear-rings; on a ledge in an opening to
l. is a crown; curtain background. Canvas, 41½ by 32 in.

40   Portrait of THE EARL OF ARUNDEL.

DUKE OF NORFOLK, K.G.

See Nos. 2 and 42.
Bust to r., looking at the spectator, in armour, bare-headed; wide
white collar; dark background; painted in an oval. Canvas,
28½ by 24½ in.

41   MARRIAGE OF ST. OATHERINE.

THE LATE DUKE OF WESTMINSTER, K.G.

> Three-quarter figure of the Virgin, seated facing the spectator,
> looking down at the Infant Saviour; He lies on her knee, look-
> ing up and holding out His l. hand to St. Catherine, who is
> bending forward in adoration with arms crossed, holding a palm;
> landscape background, with flowers and dark foliage on l.
> Canvas, 43½ by 37 in.

42   Portrait of THE EARL OF ARUNDEL.

A. J. ROBARTS, ESQ.

> See Nos. 2 and 40.
> Bust to r., looking towards the spectator; dark dress, lace ruff;
> curtain and sky background. Canvas, 21 by 19½ in.

GALLERY No. III.

OIL PAINTINGS—Nos. 43-70.

43 Portrait of THE INFANTA ISABELLA CLARA EUGENIA.

EARL OF HOPETOUN.

> Daughter of Philip II. of Spain and his 3rd wife, Elizabeth of Valois; b. 1566; m. 1597 the Archduke Albert, and became Regent of the Low Countries; at the siege of Ostend she is said to have taken an oath not to change her linen till she was mistress of that place; as the siege lasted three years, three months and three days it is not surprising that her linen at the end of the siege should have been of the colour known from that circumstance as "couleur Isabelle."
> Three-quarter figure, standing to l looking at the spectator, her hands clasped in front of her, holding the end of her black veil; she is dressed in the grey habit of the Franciscan Order of St. Clara, better known as the "Poor Clares." Canvas, 55½ by 43½ in.

44 Portrait of THE EARL OF PORTLAND.

RALPH BANKES, ESQ.

> Richard Weston, b. 1577; Ambassador to Bohemia and afterwards to Brussels; was Chancellor of the Exchequer; created Earl of Portland, 1633; Lord High Treasurer to Charles I.
> Full length, standing in front, nearly full face, his r. arm leaning on the pedestal of a column; black dress, white ruff; he wears the insignia of the Garter; in his r. hand is a letter, his l. hand, gloved, holds a wand of office; curtain and architectural background. Canvas, 82 by 53 in.

LENT BY

45   Portrait of THE COUNTESS OF SUNDERLAND.

DUKE OF DEVONSHIRE. K.G.

> Dorothea, daughter of Robert, 2nd Earl of Leicester; m. 1st,
> Henry, Earl of Sunderland; 2ndly, Robert Smythe, Esq., of
> Bounde.
> Three-quarter figure to l., standing facing the spectator; amber-
> coloured satin dress, pearl ornaments; her l. hand rests in a
> basket of roses, her r. holds back the sleeve of her gown; archi-
> tectural and curtain background. Canvas, 49 by 39½ in.

46   THE MARRIAGE OF ST. CATHERINE,

H.M. THE QUEEN.
(From Buckingham Palace.)

> Three-quarter figure of the Virgin, seated facing the spectator,
> with a wreath in her r. hand, holding on her lap the Child; He
> holds with His l. hand the r. hand of St. Catherine, who is seen
> on the r. with her emblems; in His r. hand is a ring; curtain
> and landscape background. Canvas, 49 by 46 in.

47   Portrait of ANDREA SPINOLA.

CAPTAIN HEYWOOD-LONSDALE.

> Doge of Genoa.
> Full length, seated to l. in a chair, looking at the spectator; his
> l. hand grasps the arm of the chair, his r. hand, in which is a
> paper, rests on a table beside him; red robe, white ruff; curtain
> and architectural background. Canvas, 84 by 55 in.

43   CHARITY.

LORD METHUEN.

> Three-quarter figure of a female, in white and crimson drapery
> with blue scarf, seated to r. in a landscape, bending forward and
> looking up; she holds a naked infant on her lap, and two others
> behind her are clinging to her shoulders. Canvas, 55 by 45 in.

49   Portrait of THE EARL OF STRAFFORD.

SIR PHILIP GREY EGERTON, BART.

> See No. 82.
> Three-quarter figure standing to l., looking towards the spectator
> his r. hand holds a baton, his l. is on the hilt of his sword; in
> armour, bare-headed; his helmet lies on a table behind him;
> dark background with red curtain. Canvas, 49 by 59 in.

50   Portrait of QUEEN HENRIETTA MARIA,

EARL OF CLARENDON.

See No. 20.
Full length, standing to l. on an Eastern carpet, looking towards
the spectator; her l. hand holds a fold of her skirt, the finger-
tips of the r. hand touch a table beside her, on which are a crown
and some roses in a vase; white satin dress, cut very low, pearl
ornaments, and a chain of pearls and other jewels; curtain and
architectural background; below a window on the r. is her
monogram with a crown. Canvas, 92 by 59 in.

51   Portrait of JOHN, COUNT OF NASSAU DILLENBOURG.

LORD ASHBURTON.

General of Spanish Cavalry in the service of William of Orange;
commanded the forces of the Low Countries in 1630.
Three-quarter figure, standing to l., head looking over the l.
shoulder; in armour, bare-headed; his r. hand holds a baton, his
l. a sword; curtain and architectural background. Inscribed,
" Æt. 48 A°." Canvas, 54 by 48 in.

52   Portrait of SIR EDMUND VERNEY.

SIR EDMUND VERNEY, BART.

M.P. for Wycombe in the Long Parliament; Knight Marshall, and
Standard Bearer to King Charles I.; raised the standard at
Nottingham, Aug. 25, 1642; killed at Edge Hill, Oct. 23, 1642.
Half figure standing to r., in armour, bare-headed; a baton is in his
r. hand, his l. rests on his helmet on the table beside him; long
fair hair; architectural and landscape background. Canvas,
53 by 42 in.

53   Portraits of DOROTHY, COUNTESS OF LEICESTER, AND
HER SISTER, LUCY, COUNTESS OF CARLISLE.

CHARLES MORRISON, ESQ.

Dorothy, daughter of Henry, 9th Earl of Northumberland;
m. Robert Sidney, 2nd Earl of Leicester.
Lucy, youngest daughter of above; m. James Hay, 1st Earl of
Carlisle.
Two three-quarter figures seated opposite one another, looking
towards the spectator; the one on the r. in white, with a pink
scarf round her, points with her l. hand at something in the
background; the other, in a rich red dress, holds a sprig of
orange in her l. hand and roses in her r.; both have low-necked
dresses and pearl ornaments; landscape and architectural background. Canvas 39½ by 63 in.

LENT BY

54 Portraits of LORD JOHN and LORD BERNARD STUART.

EARL OF DARNLEY.

Lord John Stuart, 4th son of Esmé, Duke of Richmond and
Lennox; b 1621: commanded the Light Horse on the King's
side in the Civil War; was killed 1644 at the battle of Alresford.

Lord Bernard Stuart, brother of above; commanded the King's
Horse Guards at Naseby and at Rowton Heath, Chester, where
he was killed in 1645.

Two full-length figures of young men, bare-headed; the one on the
r. in white satin doublet, blue cloak lined with white, and blue
hose, stands with his l. foot on a step on which his brother is
standing and looks round at the spectator; the one on the l.
stands facing the spectator in yellow doublet and crimson hose;
both have long fur hair falling over wide lace collars; dark
background. Canvas, 93 by 57 in.

55 Portraits of FIVE CHILDREN OF KING CHARLES I.

H.M. THE QUEEN.

(From Windsor Castle.)

(1) The Prince of Wales, afterwards Charles II.; (2) The Duke
of York, afterwards James II.; (3) Princess Mary, afterwards
Princess of Orange; (4) Princess Elizabeth, d. aged 13;
(5) Princess Anne, d. an infant.

Five full-length figures. In the centre Prince Charles, in a red
satin dress, faces the spectator, resting his l. hand on the head
of a large mastiff; next to him on the l. is his brother James,
in crimson, and on the extreme l. is Princess Mary, in a white
dress, standing to r., and looking round at the spectator; on the
r. is the Princess Elizabeth, in blue, standing beside a chair, on
which she holds the infant Princess Anne: at their feet lies a
spaniel; on a sideboard behind them is a flagon and a dish of
fruit.

Inscribed, " Regis magnæ Britanniæ proles—Princeps Carolus
natus 29 Maii 1630—Jacobus Dux Eboracensis natus 14 Octob.
1633—Princeps Maria nata 4 Nov. 1631—Princeps Elizabetha
nata 29 Decemb. 1635—Princeps Anna nata 17 Martii 1636."
Signed and dated, " Anton. Van Dyck eques fecit, 1637."
Canvas, 64 by 78 in.

56 Portraits of THE EARL OF BRISTOL AND
THE EARL OF BEDFORD.

EARL SPENCER, K.G.

George Digby, son of John, 1st Earl of Bristol; b. 1612; M.P. for
Dorsetshire; advised the seizure of the five members, and was
impeached; compelled to leave England in 1648; served in the

LENT BY

French wars, and afterwards under the King of Spain ; returned
after the Restoration ; impeached Lord Clarendon in 1663 ;
d. 1676.

William Russell, eldest son of Francis, 4th Earl of Bedford
became commander of the cavalry in the service of the Parliament ; fought at Edgehill ; went to the King at Oxford, and
fought at Newbury in 1643 ; was taken into custody by order
of the Parliament, and his estate sequestrated ; created Duke of
Bedford 1694 ; d. 1700.

Two full-length figures. On the r. Lord Bedford, in scarlet
uniform, with a cloak of the same colour over his r. arm ; his
helmet and cuirass are lying on the ground beside him ; his l.
hand holds a black hat. On the l. Lord Bristol, in black velvet
dress, facing the spectator, leaning his r. arm on the base of a
column ; beside him is an armillary sphere, a portfolio, and
some papers. Curtain and architectural background. Canvas,
97 by 62 in.

57   Portrait of CHARLES I. AND HIS FAMILY.

VISCOUNT GALWAY.

(1) Charles I. (see No. 20) ; (2) Queen Henrietta Maria (see
No. 20) ; (3) Prince of Wales, afterwards Charles II. ; (4)
Princess Mary, afterwards Princess of Orange.

Three-quarter figures of Charles I., seated, facing the spectator on
the l., and Queen Henrietta Maria on the r., also seated, holding the infant Princess Mary in her arms. The king's r. hand
rests on a table beside him, and at his knee is seen the little
Prince Charles ; he wears a dark dress and a blue cloak, lined
with crimson and embroidered with the Star of the Garter, of
which he wears the ribbon and badge. The Queen wears a
dress of amber silk, with white lace and pearl necklace ; behind
her are a curtain and some columns, and through an opening on
the l. are seen the Houses of Parliament, &c. Canvas, 56 by
75 in.

58 Portrait of THE EARL OF ARUNDEL AND HIS GRANDSON.

DUKE OF NORFOLK, K.G.

See Nos. 2, 40 and 42.

The grandson was probably Henry, 2nd son of Henry Frederick,
Lord Mowbray and Maltravers, by Elizabeth, daughter of the
Duke of Richmond and Lennox, who became 6th Duke of
Norfolk. :

Three-quarter figures ; Lord Arundel, bare-headed, in armour,
holding a baton in his r. hand ; his l. rests on the shoulder of
the child, who is clad in red, and holds a paper in his r. hand ;
curtain with landscape and rocks in the background. Canvas,
57 by 47 in.

LENT BY

59   Portrait of HENRIETTA OF LORRAINE.

Lord Iveagh.

Princess of Phalsburg, sister to the Duke of Lorraine.
Full length, standing to l., looking towards the spectator; black
silk robe over a white brocaded skirt, with rich lace ruff standing
up behind, and lace ruffles; pearl ear-rings and necklace; her r.
hand rests on the shoulder of a negro page, who carries a basket
of flowers; curtain on l., landscape background. Inscribed on a
label in the l.-hand corner, " Henrietta Lotharinga, Princesse de
Phalsburg, 1634," and on the other side, " Ant. Van Dyck eques
fecit." Canvas, 83 by 49½ in.

60   Portrait of THE MARCHESE DI SPINOLA.

Earl of Hopetoun.

A Genoese nobleman.
Full length, standing facing the spectator, in armour, bare-headed;
his l. hand rests on the hilt of his sword, his helmet is on the
ground beside him; curtain and architectural background; head
of a horse seen on r. Canvas, 85 by 55 in.

61   Portrait of LORD WHARTON.

H.M. The Emperor of Russia.
(From the Hermitage.)

Philip, 4th Baron Wharton; b. 1613; a violent Puritan and active
Parliamentary partisan; d. 1695.
Three-quarter figure, standing facing the spectator in a landscape,
dressed as a shepherd and holding a shepherd's staff in his l. hand;
green doublet, amber coloured mantle slung over his shoulder,
covering his r. hand which is on his hip. Canvas, 52 by 40 in.

62   Portrait of PAOLA ADORNO, MARCHESA BRIGNOLÉ-SALE.

Duke of Abercorn, K.G.

Wife of Antonio Giulio, Marchese de Brignolé-Sale, son of a Doge
of Genoa and Ambassador to Philip IV. of Spain.
Full length, standing to l. looking round towards the spectator; her
l. hand holds up her dress, her r. is held against her stomacher;
white dress embroidered with gold, pearl head-dress with plume,
grey ruff and black-edged ruffles, a ribbon is across her l.
shoulder; architectural background, with red curtain resting on
an arm-chair beside her. Canvas, 94 by 60 in.

LENT BY

63   Portrait of THE EARL OF STRAFFORD, WITH A DOG.

EARL FITZWILLIAM, K.G.

> The celebrated statesman; son of Sir W. Wentworth; b. 1593;
> was a devoted adherent of Charles I., who made him Lord
> President of the Council, Earl of Strafford, and Lord Deputy of
> Ireland 1631; was impeached of high treason and beheaded on
> Tower Hill 1641.
> Full length, standing to l. looking towards the spectator with his
> r. hand on the head of a large dog; his l. hand holds a baton;
> in armour, bare-headed; his helmet is on a pedestal near him;
> architectural and curtain background. Canvas, 89 by 55 in.

64   Portrait of THE COUNTESS OF DORSET.

LORD SACKVILLE.

> Lady Frances Cranfield, eldest daughter of Lionel, Earl of Middle-
> sex; m. Richard Sackville, 5th Earl of Dorset.
> Full length, standing to l. in a landscape, looking round at the
> spectator, and pointing to l. with her l. hand; her r. hand holds
> a scarf, which is round her; white satin dress, with blue on the
> bodice, pearl necklace and ear-rings, string of pearls in her hair.
> Canvas, 74 by 50 in.

65   Portraits of THOMAS KILLIGREW and THOMAS CAREW.

H.M. THE QUEEN.
(From Windsor Castle.)

> Thomas Killigrew, son of Sir Robert Killigrew, Chamberlain to
> the Queen; b. 1611; page of honour to Charles I.; accom-
> panied Charles II. in his exile, and was made Groom of the Bed-
> chamber after the Restoration; ambassador at Vienna, 1651;
> wrote several plays; d. 1682.
> Thomas Carew; b. 1598; Gentleman of the Privy Chamber to
> the King; author of lyric poems and sonnets; his masque,
> "Cælum Britannicum," was performed at Whitehall in 1633;
> d. 1639.
> Two three-quarter figures, seated; Killigrew on the l., facing the
> spectator, leaning his head on his l. hand, while his r. holds a
> paper; Carew on the r., with his back to the spectator, is turn-
> ing round to Killigrew and pointing with his r. hand to a paper
> which he holds in the l.; both are dressed in black and white,
> and wear their hair long: curtain and landscape background,
> with sky seen on the r. Inscribed, "A. van Dyck," and dated
> 1638. Canvas, 51 by 55¼ in.

66

Portrait of THE ABBÉ SCAGLIA.

CAPTAIN G. L. HOLFORD.

Cæsar Alexander Scaglia, Abbé de Staffarde; politician and scholar; was in the service of his sovereign, the Duke of Savoy, and in that of the King of Spain, for whom he was one of the negotiators of the Peace of Munster; established himself in the convent of the Recollets; d 1641 (?).

Ful length, standing facing the spectator, leaning his r. arm on the base of a column, and holding up his cloak with the l.; he is robed in black, with white collar and cuffs; curtain and architectural background. Canvas, 80 by 44 in.

67

RINALDO AND ARMIDA.

DUKE OF NEWCASTLE.

Illustration of the "Jerusalem Delivered" of Tasso. The Crusaders having arrived at the Holy City in order to effect its release from Pagan domination, Armida, a beautiful sorceress, is urged by the Spirit of Evil to ensnare Rinaldo and his companions.

He appears here sleeping on a bank, forgetful of his mission, while Armida, attended by cupids, bends over him and binds a wreath about him; a siren, emerging from some water on the r., sings from a scroll of music which she holds in her hand. Canvas, 93 by 88 in.

68

Portrait of BEATRICE DE CUSANCE ("MADAME DE STE. CROIX").

H.M. THE QUEEN.
(From Windsor Castle.)

Daughter of Claude François de Cusance, Baron de Beauvoir; m. 1635 Eugène Leopold, Prince de Cante-Croix, who died in 1637; she died in 1663.

Full length, standing to l., with one foot on a step, putting aside a curtain with her r. hand, and holding up her robe with the l.; dark robe over a white brocaded dress, low necked, and ornamented with strings of pearls; pearl necklace and ear-rings; a small dog is on the step; architectural and garden background Canvas, 80 by 46 in.

LENT BY

69   Portraits of THREE CHILDREN OF KING CHARLES I.

H.M. THE QUEEN.
(From Windsor Castle.)

(1) Prince of Wales; (2) Princess Mary; (3) Duke of York.
(See No. 55.)

Three full-length figures, standing facing the spectator; on the l.
Prince Charles, in amber-coloured silk, leans his elbow on a
column, standing with legs crossed; on the r. Princess Mary, in
white lace frock with blue train, her hands joined in front of her;
between them the little Duke of York, in white frock with
crimson sleeves, holds his brother's arm with both hands; on
either side is a spaniel.

Inscribed, " Regis magnæ Britanniæ proles—Princeps Carolus
natus 29 Maii 1630—Jacobus Dux Eboracensis natus 14 Octob.
1633—Et Filia Princeps Maria nata 4 Nov. 1631. Ant. Van
Dyck ft Anno Do. 1635." Canvas, 52 by 59 in.

70   Portrait of PRINCESS BALBI.

CAPTAIN G. L. HOLFORD.

A Genoese lady.

Full length, seated facing the spectator; her r. hand, resting on the
arm of the chair, holds a fan; her r. is held against her waist;
dark dress, embroidered mantle, lace ruff; dark background.
Canvas, 73 by 48 in.

GALLERY No. IV.

OIL PAINTINGS—Nos. 71-90.

71   Portrait of THE COUNTESS OF DERBY.

EARL OF DERBY, K.G.

> Charlotte, daughter of Claude de la Tremouille, Duc de Thouars, and Charlotte Brabantine de Nassau; m. 1626, James,l Lord Strange, afterwards 7th Earl of Derby; became famous for her defence of Lathom House when it was besieged in 1644 by the forces of the Parliament, and for the energetic stand she made in the Isle of Man until she was compelled to surrender it after the death in 1651 of her husband (see No. 81); d. 1663.
>
> Half figure to r., looking at the spectator; white dress cut low, with strings of pearls and jewelled girdle, pearl necklace and ear-rings; dark background. Canvas, 28 by 22½ in.

72   Equestrian Portrait of CHARLES I.

VISCOUNT BARRINGTON.

> Small full-length of the king, in armour, bareheaded, riding a white horse through an archway; in front of him walks his equerry, M. St. Antoine, carrying his helmet; over the archway is a green curtain. Canvas, 65 by 49 in.

73   Portrait of THE EARL OF DERBY.

EARL OF DERBY, K.G.

> James, 7th Earl of Derby, son of William, 2nd Earl; b. 1606; succeeded his father 1642; was a devoted adherent of Charles I.; fell into the hands of the Parliament after the battle of Worcester, and was executed at Bolton, 1651. (See also No. 81.)
>
> Bust to l., showing r. hand; in armour, bareheaded; his r. hand rests on his helmet in front of him; white collar, ribbon and badge of the Garter; long dark hair falling over his shoulders; dark background. Canvas, 28 by 22½ in.

LENT BY

74   Portrait of LADY D'AUBIGNY.

EARL OF CLARENDON.

> Catharine, daughter of Theophilus, Earl of Suffolk; m. 1st,
> George, Lord D'Aubigny, who was killed at Edgehill in 1642;
> 2ndly, James, Earl of Newburgh.
> Half figure, standing to r., looking round at the spectator; her r.
> hand holds a wreath of flowers; crimson dress, cut low; a gauze
> scarf is over her r. shoulder; pearl necklace and ear-rings; dark
> background. Canvas, 41 by 32½ in.

75   Portrait of THE DUKE OF NEWCASTLE.

DUKE OF PORTLAND.

> Eldest son of Sir Charles Cavendish; b. 1592; created Earl of
> Newcastle 1627; Governor to Charles, Prince of Wales; defeated
> Lord Fairfax at Allerton Moor; created Marquis of Newcastle
> 1643; after the defeat at Marston Moor lived at Antwerp;
> returned at the Restoration, and was made Duke of Newcastle
> 1665; d. 1676.
> Full length, standing facing the spectator; black cloak, doublet and
> hose, wide lace collar, lace cuffs, sword; his r. hand holds a
> broad-brimmed black hat; wears the insignia of the Garter;
> architectural and curtain background; landscape on r. Canvas,
> 85 by 47½ in.

76   Portrait of QUEEN HENRIETTA MARIA.

MARQUESS OF LANSDOWNE, K.G.

> See No. 20.
> Half figure, standing to l. looking at the spectator; her r. hand
> touches a crown which lies on a table beside her; her l. hand
> holds a fold of her gown between the fingers; white gown with
> lace partly covering the neck, pink ribbons, pearl necklace and
> ear-rings; a bracelet on her r. arm is passed through a ring
> which hangs from it; curtain background. Canvas, 40 by 30 in.

77   Portrait of VITELLESCHI, CHIEF OF THE JESUITS.

LORD BATTERSEA.

> Full length, standing facing the spectator, with his head turned
> to the l.; his r. arm rests on the base of a pillar, and holds a
> book with the forefinger between the leaves; his l. hand holds up
> his black robe; black dress; architectural background. Canvas,
> 79 by 47 in.

LENT BY

78   Portrait of ADMIRAL SIR JOHN MINNES.

EARL OF CLARENDON.

Son of Andrew Minnes, of Sandwich; b. 1598; Comptroller of the
Navy under Charles I.; dismissed for refusing to obey Lord
Warwick; employed in important commands after the Restoration.
Half figure, facing the spectator, head turned to l.; his r. hand,
gloved, holds a sash which crosses his breast; crimson dress,
with cuirass; long hair, fall ng over his shoulders; brown
background.   Canvas, 41 by 32½ in.

79   Portrait of THE EARL OF PETERBOROUGH.

MRS. ELRINGTON BISSET.

John Mordaunt, 5th Baron Mordaunt; created Earl of Peterborough 16⸱7; Master-General of the Ordnance under the
Commonwealth.
Full length, standing in front; his r. hand holding aside a curtain;
his l., gloved, grasps his gold embroidered baldric; red and
gold uniform, with red cloak over his l. arm; architectural
background.   Canvas, 86 by 49 in.

80 Portrait of THE PAINTER'S WIFE, AS HERMINIA PUTTING
ON CLORINDA'S ARMOUR.

JOHN C. HARFORD, ESQ.

Mary Ruthven, daughter of Patrick Ruthven, and grand-daughter
of the Earl of Gowrie, who joined in the conspiracy for seizing
on James VI. of Scotland, known as the "Raid of Ruthven."
She m. Sir Anthony Van Dyck in 1639 or 1640; soon after his
death she m. 2ndly, Sir Richard Pryce, of Goggerdam; d. 1645,
leaving a daughter by her 1st husband, Justiniana, who m. Sir
John Stepney, of Prendergaft.
Half figure, standing to l., head turned towards the spectator, the
l. hand resting on a helmet; red and white drapery, over which
is a cuirass; behind her, on a green mantle which is over her
r. shoulder, stands a Cupid; architectural and landscape background.   (See Tasso's 'Jerusalem Delivered,' vi. 91, &c.)
Canvas, 41 by 51 in.

C

LENT BY

81   Portraits of **THE EARL AND COUNTESS OF DERBY
AND THEIR DAUGHTER.**

EARL OF CLARENDON.

See Nos. 71 and 73. The daughter, Lady Catherine Stanley, m.
William Pierrepoint, Marquis of Dorchester.
Full-length figures, standing; the Earl in black, turning to l., and
pointing with his l. hand, the Countess in a white satin dress,
the bodice trimmed with pearls, flowers in her r. hand; the child
in a red frock with lace trimming; curtain and landscape background. Canvas, 96 by 82 in.

82   Portrait of **THE EARL OF STRAFFORD AND HIS
SECRETARY, SIR PHILIP MAINWARING.**

EARL FITZWILLIAM, K.G.

Thomas Wentworth, son of Sir W. Wentworth; b. 1593; was a
devoted adherent of Charles I., who made him Lord President
of the Council and Earl of Strafford; was impeached for high
treason, and beheaded on Tower Hill, 12th May, 1641.
The Earl, in black, is seated on the l. facing the spectator, resting
his arms on the elbow of his chair, and holding a letter in his
l. hand. Sir Philip Mainwaring, in red, is seated at a table on
the r. holding a pen, with a letter lying before him, and
looking round to Lord Strafford; curtain and architectural background, with landscape seen on the r. Canvas, 50 by 55 in.

83   Portrait of **VISCOUNT GRANDISON.**

DUKE OF GRAFTON, K.G.

William, son of Sir Edward Villiers; b. 1614; succeeded his
great-uncle, Sir Oliver St. John, in 1630 as 2nd Viscount
Grandison; d. 1643 of a wound received at the siege of Bristol.
Full length, standing in front; his gloved r. hand, holding his hat,
rests on his hip; his l. holds the end of the red cloak which is
over his l. arm; red and gold uniform, enormous lace collar,
buff boots; long auburn hair; landscape background. Canvas,
86 by 52½ in.

LENT BY

84   Portrait of THE EARL OF PEMBROKE.

VISCOUNT GALWAY.

> See No. 14.
> Half figure, standing facing the spectator, head turned slightly to
> r.; his r. hand holds a crimson and gold sash, which crosses his
> breast; his l. hand, gloved, is against his hip; crimson and
> white dress, with cuirass; long fair hair falling over his
> shoulders. Canvas, 42 by 32½ in.

85   THE BETRAYAL OF CHRIST.

SIR FRANCIS COOK, BART.

> In the centre of the picture Judas, wrapped in a brown cloak,
> leans towards the Saviour and grasps His hand; numerous
> figures with weapons, &c., around them; the scene is lit up by
> a torch. Canvas, 55 by 44 in.
> This picture differs from No. 30 chiefly in showing two figures
> struggling together in the l.-hand corner.

86   THE GUITAR-PLAYER.

EARL OF NORTHBROOK.

> Full-length figure of a man, seated in a room, facing the spectator,
> playing a guitar, and apparently singing; black dress, showing
> white in the sleeves, wide white collar and cuffs, buff boots;
> long dark hair falling over his shoulders. Canvas, 61 by 43 in.

87   Portrait of THE PAINTER.

DUKE OF GRAFTON, K.G.

> See notice at the beginning of the Catalogue.
> Three-quarter figure, standing to l. leaning on a pedestal; red
> dress, dark green cloak; landscape background. Canvas, 47 by
> 34 in.

88   Portrait of A GENTLEMAN.

HARRIS VALPY, ESQ.

> Half figure, standing facing the spectator, with his r. hand held
> to his breast; black satin cloak, wide white collar and cuffs;
> architectural background. Canvas, 48 by 37½ in.

89   THE MARTYRDOM OF ST. STEPHEN.

EARL EGERTON OF TATTON.

> Full length figure, less than life size, of the saint kneeling on the ground in a landscape, looking up; six figures of men stoning him ; two other figures on the r. look on ; two child angels in the air above him hold wreaths and a palm.   Canvas, 70 by 59 in.

90   Portraits of THE COUNTESS OF CARLISLE
AND HER DAUGHTER.

DUKE OF DEVONSHIRE, K.G.

> Marga.et, daughter of Francis, 4th Earl of Bedford ; m. 1st, James Hay, 2nd Earl of Carlisle (No. 119); 2ndly, Edward Montague, Earl of Manchester; 3rdly, Robert Rich, Earl of Warwick and Holland
>
> Three-quarter figure, seated to l, looking at the spectator; red dress, pearl ornaments ; her l. hand rests on the arm of the chair, her r. is on the shoulder of the child who stands at her knee. Canvas, 49 by 42 in.

GALLERY No. V.

OIL PAINTINGS—Nos. 91-111.

LENT BY

91   ANDROMEDA.

T. HUMPHRY WARD, ESQ.

Full-length nearly nude figure, with blue drapery, chained to a rock. Canvas, 84 by 51 in.

92   Portrait of LIBERTI.

DUKE OF GRAFTON, K.G.

Henry Liberti, of Groningen, organist of the Cathedral at Antwerp. Half figure, standing facing the spectator, looking to r., leaning his r. arm on the base of a column; his l. hand, holding a paper, is crossed over the r.; black gown, with gold chain; dark background. Canvas, 44 by 34 in.

93   Portrait of THE EARL OF DORSET.

LORD SACKVILLE.

Edward, 2nd son of Robert Sackville, 2nd Earl of Dorset; b. 1590; served in the Palatinate Regiment under Lord Vere; succeeded his brother Richard as 4th Earl 1624; d. 1652.

Full length, standing to l., looking at the spectator, holding a stick in his r. hand; his gloved l. hand rests on his hip; red and gold uniform, cuirass, embroidered sash round his waist, where a key hangs, wide lace collar with pink bow, order of the Garter; long brown hair; his helmet is on a pedestal beside him; curtain background. Canvas, 85 by 53 in.

LENT BY

94   Portrait of LADY BORLACE.

RALPH BANKES, ESQ.

Miss Bankes, of Kingston Lacy ; m. Sir John Borlace (No. 96).
Three-quarter figure, standing to l., three-quarter profile; her r.
hand presses a scarf at her waist, her l. holds a fold of her skirt ;
white satin gown, low necked, pearl ornaments ; a vase of
flowers stands on a pedestal in front of her. Canvas, 53 by
42 in.

95   Portraits of THE DUCHESS OF BUCKINGHAM AND HER
THREE CHILDREN.

BARON ARNOLD DE FOREST.

Catherine, daughter of Francis Manners, Lord Roos, afterwards
Earl of Rutland ; m. 1620, George, 1st Duke of Buckingham,
2nd, Randal, Marquis of Antrim.
Full-length figures. The Duchess in a black dress, seated, facing
the spectator, holding with her r. hand a miniature of her
husband, of whom a portrait is seen in the background. On the
l. stands her younger son, Lord Francis Villiers (see No. 38),
in bronze-colour and silver dress. On the r. her elder son,
George, 2nd Duke (see No. 38), dressed in red ; he holds his
mother's left hand with both his own, and looks round at his
sister Mary, afterwards created Duchess of Buckingham ; she
is dressed in white satin, with pearls. Curtain and sky background. Canvas, 95 by 76 in.

96   Portrait of SIR JOHN BORLACE.

RALPH BANKES, ESQ.

Son of Sir William Borlace, Bart., and father of Edmund Borlace,
the Irish historian.
Three-quarter figure, standing facing the spectator, leaning his
r. arm on a pedestal ; his l. hand, gloved, rests on his hip ; black
and white dress, wide lace collar, a black cloak is over his r. arm ;
long fair hair ; dark background. Canvas, 53 by 42 in.

LENT BY

97 Portrait of THE COUNTESS OF PETERBOROUGH.

Mrs. Elrington Bisset.

Elizabeth, daughter of William, Lord Effingham ; m. John, 1st Earl
of Peterborough (No. 79).
Full length, standing to l. looking at the spectator, holding by a
chain a tiger cub; her l. hand holds a fold of her skirt; amber-
coloured satin dress, cut low, pearl ornaments ; dark background.
Canvas, 85 by 48 in.

98 Portrait of SIR KENELM DIGBY.

Lord Sackville.

A distinguished soldier, scholar and courtier ; b. 1603 ; was noted
for his handsome person and extraordinary strength ; d. 1665.
Half figure, standing to l., looking at the spectator, his r. hand
held against his breast; dark dress; an armillary sphere in the
l. corner; dark background. Canvas, 41½ by 32½ in.

99 Portrait of THE DUCHESSE DE CROY.

Marquess of Lothian.

Geneviève d'Urfé, daughter of the Marquis d'Urfé ; b. about 1598 ;
m. 1st, Charles Alexander, Duc de Croy; 2nd, Guy, Marquis
d'Harcourt ; 3rd, Antoine, Comte de Mailly.
Three-quarter figure, seated to l., looking at the spectator ; her r.
hand touches a string of pearls at her waist, her l. is on the
arm of the chair ; black dress, open at the neck, with lace ruff
standing up behind, and lace cuffs; curtain background.
Canvas, 44½ by 35½ in.

100 Portrait of THE EARL OF STRAFFORD.

Duke of Portland.

See No. 49.
Full length, in armour, standing to r. in a landscape, and looking
round at the spectator ; his l. hand holds a baton, with his r.
he is pointing towards his helmet, which lies on a rock ; on the
l. is a curtain. A long inscription occupies the bottom r. hand
corner. Canvas, 86 by 53 in.

LENT BY

101   Portrait of THE EARL OF WARWICK.

EARL OF LEICESTER, K.G.

> Robert Rich, 2nd Earl; b. 1587; succeeded his father 1618; was
> Lord High Admiral under the Parliament; d. 1658.
> Full length, standing in front, nearly full face; in armour, bare-
> headed, with broad white collar; his r. arm leans on a pedestal,
> on which are his helmet and gauntlet; he holds a baton in his
> r. hand; a gold-embroidered red scarf is tied round his l. arm;
> curtain and architectural background. Canvas, 80 by 50 in.

102   Portrait of LADY BETTY SIDNEY.

THE DUKE OF RICHMOND AND GORDON.

> Three-quarter figure, seated facing the spectator; her r. hand rests
> on the arm of her chair, her l. hand holds some roses in her lap;
> blue satin dress, cut low, pearl ornaments, a dark-coloured cloak
> is over her r. shoulder; dark background, with curtain to r.
> Canvas, 46 by 37 in.

103   Portrait of THE MARQUESS OF HAMILTON.

LORD SACKVILLE.

> James, eldest son of James, 2nd Marquess of Hamilton; b. 1606;
> a close friend of Prince Charles, afterwards Charles I.; created
> Duke of Hamilton in 1643 , beheaded 1649.
> Full length, standing to r., looking at the spectator; in his r. hand
> is a wand, his l. holds a black hat; black dress, white falling
> collar, buff boots and gloves; he wears the Order of the Garter
> and a blue ribbon on his l. leg. Inscribed on a label in r. corner,
> "Jacobus Marchio Hamiltonia. Ætatis suæ An. Dm. 1632."
> Architectural and landscape background. Canvas, 85 by 50 in.

104   TANCRED AND HERMINIA.

EARL FITZWILLIAM, K.G.

> Scene from Tasso's 'Jerusalem Delivered.' The composition of
> this picture is similar to that of No. 67 with the figures reversed.
> Canvas, 57 by 79 in.

LENT BY

105 Portraits of THE CHILDREN OF THE EARL OF STRAFFORD.

EARL FITZWILLIAM, K.G.

William, afterwards 2nd Earl of Strafford. Anne, m. Edward, Earl of Rockingham. Arabella, m. Justin McCarthy, son of the Earl of Clancarty.
Three full-length figures, standing facing the spectator; on the r. William Wentworth, in black dress, with lace collar and cuffs and buff boots, his r. hand held in front of him; next to him is the younger girl in blue, holds the arm of the elder sister, who is seen on the l. in white satin with gold buttons; behind them is a curtain and a glimpse of the sky on the l. Canvas, 81 by 63 in.

106   A BACCHANALIAN SCENE.

LORD BELPER.

A group of naked children passing through a landscape, one of them asleep on the back of a leopard; behind is the figure of a man carrying pomegranates. Canvas, 55 by 75 in.

107   Portrait of ANNA MARIA DE SCHODT.

MESSRS. LAWRIE & Co.

Full length, standing facing the spectator, but turned slightly to l.; her hands crossed in front of her; the r. holds a handkerchief; dark dress, with embroidered bodice and lace cuffs, stiff ruff; curtain and landscape background. Canvas, 71 by 46 in.

108   Portrait of MARGARET OF LORRAINE.

HENRY PFUNGST, ESQ.

B. 1613; m. Gaston, Duc d'Orléans (No. 164); d. 1672.
Half figure to r., looking at the spectator; dark dress, with white satin stomacher and sleeves; pink bows, lace ruff standing out behind, pearl necklace; dark background. Canvas, 28½ by 24 in. (painted in an oval).

109   JUPITER AND ANTIOPE.

EDWARD F. PYE-SMITH, ESQ.

> Nearly nude figure of Antiope asleep, with Jupiter in the form of
> a satyr bending over her.   Canvas, 43½ by 58 in.

110   AN ALLEGORY.

SIR CHARLES TURNER.

> Nude figure of a Cupid, sitting on a stone slab, on which are
> flowers and books; he is looking sorrowfully on the ground in
> front of him, where are to be seen various articles, among them
> a skull, a sceptre, a flag, &c.; smoke is rising from an urn
> behind him; on a paper is written, "Defecerunt sicut in fumo,"
> &c.   The flowers are by Seghers.   Canvas, 43½ by 33½ in.

111   Portrait of THE MARQUESS OF MONTROSE (?).

MARQUESS OF BRISTOL.

> James Graham; b. 1612; created Marquess of Montrose 1644;
> was commander-in-chief of the King's forces in Scotland and
> gained many victories over the Covenanters, but was defeated
> at Philiphaugh and retired abroad; returning later on he was
> made prisoner and executed at Edinburgh in 1650.
> Half figure to l., looking at the spectator; in armour, bare-headed;
> red sash round his waist; dark background.   Canvas, 30 by
> 25½ in.

GALLERY No. VI.

OIL PAINTINGS—Nos. 112-129.

LENT BY

112

Portrait of THE COUNTESS OF CLANBRASSIL.

EARL OF DENBIGH.

Anne Carey, daughter of Henry, Earl of Monmouth; m., 1st, James Hamilton, 2ndly, Sir Robert Maxwell, Bart., Viscount Clandeboye, raised in 1647 to the Earldom of Clanbrassil; her younger sister, Mary, m. William, 3rd Earl of Denbigh.

Full length, standing to l. in a landscape, head turned towards the spectator; blue low-cut dress, pearl ornaments; she is holding a cloak. Canvas, 83 by 49½ in.

113

Portrait of A LADY.

EARL OF DENBIGH.

Hitherto erroneously supposed to be a portrait of Lady Elizabeth Feilding, 3rd daughter of 1st Earl of Denbigh, who m. 1639, Lewis Viscount Boyle, of Kynalmeaky, was afterwards created Countess of Guildford, 1660, in her own right, and d. 1673.

Three-quarter figure, seated to l, looking at the spectator, her l. hand resting on the arm of the chair; dark gold embroidered dress, high stiff ruff. Canvas, 58 by 42½ in.

114

Portrait of THE DUKE OF HAMILTON.

EARL OF DENBIGH.

James, 1st Duke of Hamilton, K.G., b. 1606; m. Lady Mary Feilding (No. 116), daughter of 1st Earl of Denbigh, created Duke 1643; defeated at Preston by Cromwell, and taken prisoner; executed in New Palace Yard, 1649.

Full length, standing to r., looking at the spectator, holding his hat in his r. hand; dark blue dress, black cloak and wide falling lace collar; wearing the insignia of the Order of the Garter. Canvas, 82 by 49½ in.

115   THE CRUCIFIXION.

REV. LANGTON GEORGE VERE.

> Christ on the cross ; the Virgin and St. John standing at the foot
> of the cross on the l. ; Mary Magdalene kneeling in adoration on
> the r. ; boy angels in the sky above. Canvas, 118 by 86¼ in.

116   Portrait of LADY MARY FEILDING.

EARL OF DENBIGH.

> Eldest daughter of William, 1st Earl of Denbigh, and Susan
> Villiers, sister of George, 1st Duke of Buckingham ; b. 1613 ;
> m. James, 1st Duke of Hamilton (No. 114) ; d. 1638.
> Full length, standing to r., looking at the spectator ; dark blue
> low-cut satin dress, trimmed with fur, pearl ornaments ; her r.
> hand hangs by her side, her l. is raised to her waist; a small
> dog runs in front of her ; architectural and landscape back-
> ground. Canvas, 83 by 47 in.

117   Portrait of KING CHARLES I.

EARL OF DENBIGH.

> See No. 20.
> Three-quarter figure, standing in front, facing the spectator, in
> armour, bare-headed ; his r. hand rests on his helmet, in his l. is
> a baton ; curtain and sky background. Canvas, 48 by 38 in.

118   Portrait of CHARLES DE MALORY or MALLERY.

EARL COWPER, K.G.

> A celebrated engraver; b. at Antwerp at the end of the 15th
> century.
> Half figure to r., head turned over the r. shoulder, his l. hand
> raised to his breast ; dark background, with column on r. Canvas,
> 48 by 36 in.

119   Portrait of THE EARL OF CARLISLE.

VISCOUNT COBHAM.

> James Hay, son of James, 1st Earl, by Honora, daughter of Lord
> Denny ; succeeded his father 1636 ; d. 1660.
> Full length, standing to r. ; his r. hand, gloved, hangs by his side ;
> dark blue dress and cloak, wide lace falling collar ; architectural
> and landscape background. Canvas, 80¼ by 50 in.

LENT BY

120   THE CRUCIFIXION.

PRIOR PARK COLLEGE, BATH.

> Christ on the cross; the Virgin and St. John standing at the foot
> of the cross on the l.; Mary Magdalene kneeling in adoration on
> the r. Canvas, 82 by 70 in. (arched top).

121   Portrait of THE DUCHESS OF RICHMOND.

MARQUESS OF BATH.

> Frances Howard, daughter of Thomas Howard, Viscount Bindon;
> b. about 1578; m. 1st, Henry Crannel, son of an Alderman of
> London; 2ndly, Edward Seymour, Earl of Hertford; 3rdly,
> Ludovick Stuart, Duke of Richmond, and survived them all;
> died 1639.
> Full length, standing to l.; low black dress and veil; holds in her
> r. hand a long stick, her l. rests on a table on which are a coronet
> and a bell; long inscription and date, 1633. Canvas, 85½ by 49 in.

122   Portrait of MONSIEUR FRANCOIS LANGLOIS,
                    called DE CHARTRES.

W. GARNETT, ESQ.

> A bookseller and publisher, called "De Chartres" from his native
> town; fond of art, and a skilled musician; he was a great friend
> and companion of Van Dyck, who probably painted this portrait
> during his visit to Paris in 1625, just after his return from
> Italy.
> Half figure, in fancy dress of red, with broad-brimmed hat, play-
> ing bag-pipes; in the l. corner is seen the head of a dog;
> architectural and sky background. Canvas, 40 by 32¼.

123   Portrait of LORD CAPEL.

EARL OF CLARENDON.

> Arthur Capel, only son of Sir Henry Capel, created Baron Capel
> 1641; was a zealous adherent of Charles I.; beheaded 9th March,
> 1648-9.
> Half figure, slightly to r., head turned to l., looking at the spec-
> tator; buff jacket, steel gorget: dark background. Canvas,
> 29 by 24 in.

LENT BY

124   Portrait of PRINCE D'ANGRI.

GEORGE SALTING, ESQ.

Half figure, standing to l., three-quarter profile; he is wrapped in
a long black cloak, which only leaves visible his lace collar;
his gloved l. hand rests on the hilt of his sword; architectural
background. Canvas, 49 by 37 in.

125   Portrait of THE EARL OF NORTHUMBERLAND.

EARL OF DENBIGH.

Henry Percy, 9th Earl, son of Henry, 8th Earl, and Catherine
Neville, daughter of Lord Latimer; imprisoned for fifteen years
by James I. on suspicion of complicity in the Gunpowder Plot;
m. Dorothy Devereux, sister of Robert, Earl of Essex, and
widow of Sir Thomas Perrot; d. 1632.
Half figure, seated to l., leaning his head on his r. arm, which
rests on a table; dark dress; brown curtain background.
Canvas, 29½ by 24½ in.

126   Portrait of QUEEN HENRIETTA MARIA.

EARL OF DENBIGH.

See No. 20.
Half figure to r., in profile; white dress and cloak, blue bow;
brown background. Canvas, 29½ by 24½ in.

127   Portrait of THE COUNTESS OF SOUTHAMPTON.

EARL COWPER, K.G.

Elizabeth, daughter of Francis Leigh, Earl of Chichester; m. as
his second wife, Thomas Wriothesley, 4th Earl of Southampton.
Full length, seated to l., her r. arm resting on a pedestal, three-
quarter profile; white dress, blue cloak, thrown across her lap;
architectural and landscape background. Canvas, 87 by 51 in.

128   Portrait of KING CHARLES I.

EARL OF DENBIGH.

> See No. 20.
> Half length to l., three-quarter profile; black dress with wide
>   falling lace collar, insignia of the Order of the Garter; dark
>   background. Canvas, 29½ by 24½ in.

129   Portrait of THE EARL OF KINNOUL.

EARL OF CLARENDON.

> George Hay, 2nd Earl; Captain of the Yeomen of the Guard to
>   Charles I., and one of his most devoted adherents; d. 1644.
> Full length, standing to r., three-quarter profile; in armour, bare-
>   headed, his mailed r. hand holds a baton, while his l., uncovered,
>   rests on a table covered with a red cloth, on which lies his helmet;
>   dark background. Canvas, 85 by 50¾ in.

WATER COLOUR ROOM.

SKETCHES IN OIL AND DRAWINGS—
Nos. 130–235.

The forty portraits in grisaille (**Nos. 139–158** and **161–180**), lent by the Duke of Buccleuch, formed a portion of the series of portraits by Van Dyck of eminent men of his time, some of which he etched himself, and others were reproduced by the best engravers of the day. He conceived the idea of this work when in Italy, and worked at it assiduously during the rest of his life. A publisher of Antwerp, Martin Van den Enden, was the person to whom he entrusted the business part of the undertaking. At Van Dyck's death, eighty-four portraits had been issued. Three or four years afterwards, Giles Hendricx, who appears to have acquired the plates, published a volume of one hundred portraits, to which he gave the name of "The Inconography of Van Dyck." The frontispiece of this work was adorned with a portrait of Van Dyck, and on the pedestal was the following inscription: "Icones principum, virorum doctorum, pictorum, chalcographorum, statuariorum nec non amatorum pictoriæ artis numero centum ab Antonio Van Dyck pictore ad vivum expressæ eivsq : sumptibus æri incisæ. Antverpiæ, Gillis Hendricx excudit anno 1645." A second edition of this work contained one hundred and eight portraits. Another Antwerp publisher, Jean Meyssens, added a few more portraits to an edition which he published some years later; and at the beginning of the eighteenth century, the volume contained one hundred and twenty-eight plates, the originals of which were purchased for the Louvre in 1851.

LENT BY

130 PORTRAITS OF ELIZABETH OF FRANCE, QUEEN OF SPAIN, AND HER
     TWO CHILDREN. Oil. Panel, 12 by 8½ in.

M. LÉON BONNAT.

131 THE ADORATION OF THE SHEPHERDS. Oil. Panel, 22 by 16 in.

M. HUYBRECHTS.

132 PORTRAIT OF THE DUC D'EPERNON ON HORSEBACK. Sepia,
     heightened with white. Panel, 12½ by 9 in.

EARL OF PEMBROKE.

133 PORTRAIT OF ALBERT, COMTE D'AREMBERG, ON HORSEBACK. Water
     colour. 15¾ by 12 in.

J. P. HESELTINE, ESQ.

134 THE RAISING OF THE CROSS. Oil. Canvas, 27½ by 51 in.

CAPTAIN G. L. HOLFORD.

135 A SOLDIER ON HORSEBACK. Oil. Canvas, 14 by 9½ in.

JAMES KNOWLES, ESQ.

136 PORTRAIT OF THE INFANTA ISABELLA CLARA EUGENIA. (See also
     Nos. 43 and 152.) Panel, 9½ by 7½ in.

M. LÉON BONNAT.

137 THE RAISING OF THE CROSS. Oil. Panel, 10¼ by 8½ in.

M. LÉON BONNAT.

138 PORTRAIT OF HENDRICK VAN BALEN. Panel, 8¾ by 7¼ in.

M. LÉON BONNAT.

139 PORTRAIT OF KING CHARLES I. Panel, 8½ by 7½ in.

DUKE OF BUCCLEUCH, K.G.

D

LENT BY

140 UNKNOWN PORTRAIT. Panel. 9 by 6¾ in.
DUKE OF BUCCLEUCH, K.G.

141 PORTRAIT OF ADRIAN STALBENT, PAINTER. (See also No. 185.)
Panel, 8¾ by 6¾ in.
DUKE OF BUCCLEUCH, K.G.

142 PORTRAIT OF HENRI GODEFREY, COMTE DE PAPPENHEIM. Panel,
8½ by 6¾ in.
DUKE OF BUCCLEUCH, K.G.

143 PORTRAIT OF THE CARDINAL ARCHDUKE FERDINAND, REGENT OF
THE LOW COUNTRIES. (See also No. 36.) Panel, 8¼ by 7 in.
DUKE OF BUCCLEUCH, K.G.

144 PORTRAIT OF CORNELIUS VAN DER GEEST, COLLECTOR OF WORKS
OF ART. Panel, 8¾ by 6½ in.
DUKE OF BUCCLEUCH, K.G.

145 PORTRAIT OF CHARLES DE COLONNA, SPANISH GENERAL. Panel,
9 by 6½ in.
DUKE OF BUCCLEUCH, K.G.

146 PORTRAIT OF FRANS FRANCK or FRANCKEN, PAINTER. Panel,
8¼ by 6¾ in.
DUKE OF BUCCLEUCH, K.G.

147 PORTRAIT OF ADRIAN BROUWER, PAINTER. Panel, 8¼ by 6½ in.
DUKE OF BUCCLEUCH, K.G.

148 PORTRAIT OF PAUL PONTIUS, LINE ENGRAVER. Panel, 9¾ by
7½ in.
DUKE OF BUCCLEUCH, K.G.

149 PORTRAIT OF FRANCIS DE MONCADA, MARQUIS D'AYTONE. Panel,
9½ by 6½ in.
DUKE OF BUCCLEUCH, K.G.

LENT BY

150 PORTRAIT OF DON EMANUEL FROOKAS, CONDE DE FERIA. Panel, 8 by 6 in.

DUKE OF BUCCLEUCH, K.G.

151 PORTRAIT OF FREDERIC HENRY, PRINCE OF ORANGE AND COUNT OF NASSAU. Panel, $8\frac{3}{4}$ by $6\frac{1}{2}$ in.

DUKE OF BUCCLEUCH, K.G.

152 PORTRAIT OF THE INFANTA ISABELLA CLARA EUGENIA. (See Nos. 43 and 136.) Panel, 9 by $6\frac{3}{4}$ in.

DUKE OF BUCCLEUCH, K.G.

153 PORTRAIT OF JAN VAN RAVENSTEIN, PAINTER. Panel, $9\frac{1}{2}$ by $6\frac{3}{4}$ in.

DUKE OF BUCCLEUCH, K.G.

154 PORTRAIT OF DON AMBROSE SPINOLA, DUKE OF SAN SEVERINO, CAPTAIN-GENERAL OF SPAIN. Panel, $9\frac{1}{4}$ by $6\frac{3}{4}$ in.

DUKE OF BUCCLEUCH, K.G.

155 PORTRAIT OF ALVAREZ BASAN, MARQUIS DE ST. CROIX, SPANISH ADMIRAL. Panel, 9 by 6 in.

DUKE OF BUCCLEUCH, K.G.

156 PORTRAIT OF ANDREAS COLYNS DE NOLE, SCULPTOR. Panel, $9\frac{1}{4}$ by $6\frac{1}{4}$ in.

DUKE OF BUCCLEUCH, K.G.

157 PORTRAIT OF GENEVIÈVE D'ORFÉ, DUCHESSE DE CROY. (See No. 99.) Panel, $9\frac{1}{2}$ by $6\frac{3}{4}$ in.

DUKE OF BUCCLEUCH, K.G.

158 PORTRAIT OF MARTIN PEPYN, PAINTER. Panel, $8\frac{3}{4}$ by 7 in.

DUKE OF BUCCLEUCH, K.G.

159 THE ECSTASY OF ST. AUGUSTINE. Panel, $19\frac{1}{2}$ by $11\frac{1}{2}$ in.

EARL OF NORTHBROOK.

LENT BY

160 PORTRAIT OF ADAM DE COSTER, PAINTER. (See also No. 168.)
Panel, 9½ by 7½ in.

G. A. STOREY, ESQ., A.R.A.

161 PORTRAIT OF ANTONY CORNELISSEN, COLLECTOR OF WORKS OF
ART. (See also No. 184.) Panel, 9¾ by 6 in.

DUKE OF BUCCLEUCH, K.G.

162 PORTRAIT OF SIMON DE VOS, PAINTER. Panel, 8¼ by 5¾ in.

DUKE OF BUCCLEUCH, K.G.

163 PORTRAIT OF CHARLES DE MALLERY, OR MALORY, ENGRAVER. (See
also No. 118.) Panel, 8½ by 6 in.

DUKE OF BUCCLEUCH, K.G.

164 PORTRAIT OF GASTON, DUC D'ORLEANS. Panel, 9½ by 7 in.

DUKE OF BUCCLEUCH, K.G.

165 PORTRAIT OF EMILIE DE SOLMS, PRINCESS OF ORANGE. Panel,
9¼ by 6¾ in.

DUKE OF BUCCLEUCH, K.G.

166 PORTRAIT OF PETER STEVENS, GRAND ALMONER OF ANTWERP,
COLLECTOR OF WORKS OF ART. Panel, 9 by 6 in.

DUKE OF BUCCLEUCH, K.G.

167 PORTRAIT OF WILHELMUS WOLFGANG, COUNT PALATINE OF THE
RHINE, DUKE OF BAVARIA. Panel, 9½ by 6½ in.

DUKE OF BUCCLEUCH, K.G.

168 PORTRAIT OF ADAM DE COSTER, PAINTER. (See also No. 160.)
Panel, 9¼ by 6 in.

DUKE OF BUCCLEUCH, K.G.

169 PORTRAIT OF GASPAR DE CRAYER, PAINTER. Panel, 9 by 7 in.

DUKE OF BUCCLEUCH, K.G.

LENT BY

170 PORTRAIT OF THE PAINTER. Panel, 9 by 6 in.

DUKE OF BUCCLEUCH, K.G.

171 PORTRAIT OF SIR PETER PAUL RUBENS, PAINTER. (See also
No. 176.) Panel, 9¾ by 7 in.

DUKE OF BUCCLEUCH, K.G.

172 PORTRAIT OF DON DIEGO DE GUZMAN, MARQUIS DE LEGANES.
Panel, 8½ by 6 in.

DUKE OF BUCCLEUCH, K.G.

173 PORTRAIT OF HENDRICK VAN BALEN, PAINTER. (See also No. 138.)
Panel, 8½ by 5½ in.

DUKE OF BUCCLEUCH, K.G. .

174 PORTRAIT OF ART WOLFART, PAINTER. Panel, 8½ by 6 in.

DUKE OF BUCCLEUCH, K.G.

175 PORTRAIT OF PETER DE JODE, LINE ENGRAVER.   Panel,
8¼ by 7 in.

DUKE OF BUCCLEUCH, K.G.

176 PORTRAIT OF SIR PETER PAUL RUBENS, PAINTER. (See also
No. 171.) Panel, 7¾ by 6½ in.

DUKE OF BUCCLEUCH, K.G.

177 PORTRAIT OF SEBASTIAN VRANCX, PAINTER. Panel, 9 by 6 in.

DUKE OF BUCCLEUCH, K.G.

178 PORTRAIT OF NICOLAS FABRICIUS DE PEIRESE, SCHOLAR AND
COLLECTOR OF WORKS OF ART. Panel, 8 by 6 in.

DUKE OF BUCCLEUCH, K.G.

179 PORTRAIT OF JUSTUS LIPSIUS, HISTORIAN. Panel, 8¼ by 5¾ in.

DUKE OF BUCCLEUCH, K.G.

☰ LENT BY

180 PORTRAIT OF GASPAR GEVARTIUS, LAWYER AND MAN OF LETTERS.
Panel, 8¼ by 6½ in.

DUKE OF BUCCLEUCH, K.G.

181 PORTRAIT OF PRINCE WILLIAM OF ORANGE WHEN A BOY. Black
chalk. 10 by 7¼ in.

GEORGE SALTING, ESQ.

182 THREE SKETCHES IN ONE PANEL. (1) HEAD OF THE VIRGIN,
2¼ by 1¾ in. (2) VIRGIN AND CHILD AND ST. JOSEPH,
4½ by 5¼ in. (3) VIRGIN AND CHILD, 5 by 2¾ in.

J. P. HESELTINE, ESQ.

183 RINALDO AND ARMIDA. (See No. 67.) Pen and bistre,
heightened with white. 9¾ by 13½ in.

SIR J. C. ROBINSON.

184 SAINT CATHERINE OF ALEXANDRIA, ST. GEORGE, ST. JEROME,
AND OTHER SAINTS : DESIGN FOR AN ALTAR-PIECE. Bistre.
12 by 7¾ in.

GEORGE SALTING, ESQ.

185 PORTRAIT OF ADRIAN STALBENT, PAINTER. (See also No. 141.)
Red chalk. 8½ by 6½ in.

J. P. HESELTINE, ESQ.

186 THE ENTOMBMENT. Oil on paper. 10¾ by 7¾ in.

SIR J. C. ROBINSON.

187 PORTRAIT OF LADY RITCHIE. Black chalk. 14 by 9½ in.

J. P. HESELTINE, ESQ.

188 STUDY OF HEADS. Red chalk. 7¼ by 7 in.

JAMES KNOWLES, ESQ.

LENT BY

189 THE CRUCIFIXION. Oil on paper. 11¾ by 7¼ in.

SIR J. C. ROBINSON.

190 PORTRAIT OF LUCAS VORSTERMANN, ENGRAVER. Pencil and chalk. 9¾ by 7 in.

J. P. HESELTINE, ESQ.

191 A SIAMESE AMBASSADOR TO THE COURT OF ST. JAMES. Black chalk, washed with colour. 17½ by 10 in.

HENRY HOBHOUSE, ESQ., M.P.

192 BACCHANALIAN SCENE. Pen and bistre. 6¼ by 8½ in.

J. P. HESELTINE, ESQ.

193 A HEAD. Pencil. 4¾ by 3½ in.

J. P. HESELTINE, ESQ.

194 PORTRAIT OF ANTONY CORNELISSEN. (See also No. 161.) Black chalk. 8 by 6½ in.

M. LÉON BONNAT.

195 AN ENTOMBMENT. Pen and bistre. 8¾ by 11 in.

M. LÉON BONNAT.

196 PORTRAIT OF DANIEL MYTENS, PAINTER. Black chalk. 8½ by 7¼ in.

M. LÉON BONNAT.

197 STUDY OF ARMOUR. Black chalk, slightly washed. 16¾ by 10¼ in.

HENRY PFUNGST, ESQ.

198 HEAD OF CHRIST. Black chalk, heightened with white. 8 by 10 in.

M. LÉON BONNAT.

LENT BY

199 THE GOOD SAMARITAN. Pen and bistre. 9¼ by 8 in.

M. LÉON BONNAT.

200 PORTRAIT OF JEAN BAPTISTE BARBÉ, ENGRAVER. Pencil. 9½ by 7¼ in.

M. LÉON BONNAT.

201 STUDY OF ARMOUR. Black chalk washed with colour. 15½ by 9 in.

J. P. HESELTINE, ESQ.

202 HEAD OF AN OLD MAN. Pen and bistre. 8¾ by 6¼ in.

M. LÉON BONNAT.

203 STUDY OF TWO HEADS (MAN AND WOMAN). Pen and bistre, 3¾ by 5 in.

M. LÉON BONNAT.

204 THE CRUCIFIXION OF ST. PETER. Study for the picture in the Brussels Museum. Red chalk and sepia. 9 by 13¾ in.

M. H. SPIELMAN, ESQ.

205 SKETCH OF A HORSE'S LEG. Chalk. 9¼ by 6 in.

GEORGE SALTING, ESQ.

206 VENUS TRYING TO DETAIN ADONIS FROM THE CHASE. Pen and bistre, washed. 10¼ by 7¼ in.

GEORGE SALTING, ESQ.

207 CHRIST ON THE WAY TO CALVARY. Black chalk. 7¾ by 6½ in.

JAMES KNOWLES, ESQ.

208 VICTORY CROWNING A WARRIOR ON HORSEBACK, WHO IS TRAMPLING ON DISCORD AND FURY. Pen and bistre. 8½ by 7¼.

GEORGE SALTING, ESQ.

LENT BY

209 PORTRAIT GROUP. Black chalk. 10 by 8½ in.

J. P. HESELTINE, ESQ.

210 PORTRAIT OF CORNELIUS VAN DE GOES. Pen and chalk.
    9 by 7¼ in.

H.M. THE KING OF ITALY.

211 CHRIST HEALING THE PARALYTIC. Pen and bistre, washed.
    11 by 7½ in.

H.M. THE KING OF ITALY.

212 PORTRAIT OF A MAN. Black chalk. 12½ by 9¾ in.

H.M. THE KING OF ITALY.

213 CHARLES V. ON HORSEBACK. Pen and chalk. 12 by 8¾ in.

H.M. THE KING OF ITALY.

214 CHRIST BEARING THE CROSS. Pen and bistre, washed. 6 by 8 in.

H.M. THE KING OF ITALY.

215 PORTRAIT OF A YOUNG LADY. Black chalk, washed. 12¾ by 8½ in.

H.M. THE KING OF ITALY.

216 A HORSE. STUDY FOR A PORTION OF THE PICTURE OF CHARLES I.
    ON HORSEBACK AT WINDSOR CASTLE. (See No. 72.) Black
    chalk. 11½ by 7½ in.

H.M. THE QUEEN.
(From Windsor Castle.)

217 SAMSON AND DELILAH. Water colour. 15½ by 19¾ in.

J. P. HESELTINE, ESQ.

218 ECCE HOMO. Black chalk. 14¼ by 10½ in.

H.M. THE KING OF ITALY.

LENT BY!

219 PYRAMUS AND THISBE. Pen and bistre, washed. 11¾ by 7 in.
H.M. THE KING OF ITALY.

220 VENUS AND CUPID. Pen and wash. 8½ by 6¼ in.
H.M. THE KING OF ITALY.

221 PORTRAIT OF PHILIP, EARL OF PEMBROKE. (See also No. 14.)
Pen, heightened with white. 9½ by 7 in.
H.M. THE KING OF ITALY.

222 PORTRAIT OF KING CHARLES I. Pen and bistre. 11½ by 8¾ in.
H.M. THE KING OF ITALY.

223 PORTRAIT OF A MAN. Pen and bistre. 9¾ by 7¼ in.
H.M. THE KING OF ITALY.

224 SKETCH FOR RINALDO AND ARMIDA. Pen and bistre. 12 by
9¼ in.
JAMES KNOWLES, ESQ.

225 THE THREE ANGELS ENTERTAINED BY ABRAHAM. Oil on paper.
8¾ by 12¼ in.
JAMES KNOWLES, ESQ.

226 LANDSCAPE. Water colour. 11 by 7¼ in.
J. P. HESELTINE, ESQ.

227 VIRGIN AND CHILD. Bistre. 9¼ by 6¼ in.
SIR J. C. ROBINSON.

228 PORTRAIT OF KING CHARLES I. Chalk. 15¼ by 10¼ in.
SIR J. C. ROBINSON.

229 HOLY FAMILY. Pen and bistre. 4 by 3 in.
GEORGE CLAUSEN, ESQ., A.R.A.

LENT BY

230 Landscape. Water colour. 7 by 8½ in.

Sir J. C. Robinson.

231 Sketch for the Picture of the Brazen Serpent. Pen and bistre washed. 7½ by 8¾ in.

M. Léon Bonnat.

232 Procession of King Charles I. and the Knights of the Garter. Oil. Panel, 11 by 51 in.

Sketch, in grisaille, for a portion of the proposed decoration of the walls of the banqueting hall at Whitehall, the ceiling of which had been painted by Rubens. Van Dyck's idea was to represent the history of the Order of the Garter in a series of designs, of which the principal were to be: The Institution of the Order by Edward III., the Procession of the Knights in their robes, the ceremony of Installation, and the Banquet. These designs were to be carried out in tapestry. The scheme however was too costly, and the project was abandoned.

Duke of Rutland, K.G.

233 Rape of the Sabines. Oil. Canvas, 27 by 67 in.

Earl Cowper, K.G.

234 Portrait of the Countess of Bristol. Oil. Canvas, 15½ by 12¼ in.

Sir Edmund Verney, Bart.

235 Diana in the Chase. Oil. Panel, 10½ by 15½ in.

P. Heseltine, Esq.

INDEX OF

NAMES OF THE CONTRIBUTORS OF WORKS.

H.M. THE QUEEN, 38, 46, 55, 65, 68, 69, 216
H.M. THE EMPEROR OF RUSSIA, 61
H.M. THE KING OF ITALY, 210-215, 218-223

Abercorn, The Duke of, K.G., 62
Ashburton, Lord, 51

Bankes, Ralph, Esq., 44, 94, 96
Barrington, Viscount, 72
Bath, The Marquess of, 121
Battersea, Lord, 77
Belper, Lord, 106
Bisset, Mrs. Elrington, 79, 97
Bonnat, M. Léon, 130, 136-138, 194-196, 198-200, 202, 203, 231
Bristol, The Marquess of, 13, 111
Brownlow, The Earl, 11, 34
Buccleuch, The Duke of, K.G., 10, 16, 18, 139-158, 161-180
Bute, The Marquess of, 6

Chambers, Captain, 9
Clarendon, The Earl of, 33, 36, 50, 74, 78, 81, 123, 129
Clausen, George, Esq., A.R.A., 229
Cobham, Viscount, 119
Cook, Sir Francis, Bart., 85
Cowper, The Earl, K.G., 5, 118, 127, 233

Darnley, The Earl of, 54
De Forest, Baron Arnold, 95
Denbigh, The Earl of, 29, 31, 112-14, 116, 117, 125, 126, 128

Derby, The Earl of, K.G., 71, 73
Devonshire, The Duke of, K.G., 28, 32, 45, 90
Dobie, J. T., Esq., 27

Egerton of Tatton, The Earl, 89
Egerton, Sir Philip Grey, Bart., 49
Essex, The Earl of, 3

Fitzwilliam, The Earl, K.G., 12, 19, 21, 63, 82, 104, 105

Galway, Viscount, 57, 84
Garnett, William, Esq., 122
Grafton, The Duke of, K.G., 20, 83, 87, 92

Hanbury, Mrs. Culling, 4
Harford, John C., Esq., 80
Heseltine, J. P., Esq., 133, 182, 185, 187, 190, 192, 193, 201, 209, 217, 226, 235
Heywood-Lonsdale, Captain, 47
Hobhouse, Henry, Esq., M.P., 191
Holford, Captain G. L., 22, 66, 70, 134
Hopetoun, The Earl of, 43, 60
Huybrechts, M. Edmond, 131

Iveagh, Lord, 59

Knowles, James, Esq., 135, 188, 207, 224, 225

Lansdowne, The Marquess of, K.G., 76
Lawrie & Co., Messrs., 107

Leicester, The Earl of, K.G.. 101
Lothian, The Marquess of, 90

Makins, Henry F., Esq., 26
Methuen, Lord, 30, 48
Montagu, Sir Samuel, Bart., M.P., 8
Morrison, Charles, Esq , 53

Newcastle, The Duke of, 67
Norfolk, The Duke of, K.G., 15, 37, 40, 58
Normanton, The Earl of, 1, 23
Northbrook, The Earl of, 86, 159

Pembroke, The Earl of, 14, 132
Pfungst, Henry, Esq., 108, 197
Portland, The Duke of, 75, 100
Prior Park College, Bath, Trustees of, 120
Pye-Smith, Edward F., Esq., 109

Richmond and Gordon, The Duke of, K.G.,
  17, 102
Robarts, A. J., Esq., 42
Robinson, Sir J. C., 183, 186, 189, 227, 228,
  230

Rothschild, Lady de, 24
Rutland, The Duke of, K.G., 232

Sackville, Lord, 64, 93, 98, 103
Salting, George, Esq., 124, 181, 184, 205, 206,
  208
Sanders, Alfred J., Esq., 25
Spencer, The Earl, K.G., 56
Spielmann, M. H., Esq., 204
Storey, G. A., Esq., A.R.A., 160
Sutherland, The Duke of, 2, 7

Turner, Sir Charles, K.C.I.E., 110

Valpy, Harris, Esq., 88
Vere, The Rev. Langton George, 115
Verney, Sir Edmund, Bart., 52, 234

Wantage, Lord, 39
Ward, T. Humphry, Esq., 91
Westminster, The late Duke of, K.G., 35,
  41

www.ingramcontent.com/pod-product-compliance
Lightning Source LLC
Chambersburg PA
CBHW021633270326
41931CB00008B/1006